THE DAILY BETTER

365 Reasons for Optimism

HENRY EDWARDS

AUTHORS PLACE
—PRESS—

Published by Authors Place Press
9885 Wyecliff Drive, Suite 200
Highlands Ranch, CO 80126
AuthorsPlace.com

Manufactured in the United States of America.

ISBN: 978-1-62865-643-5

For Marissa and Sofie

ACKNOWLEDGMENTS

I'm grateful to live in the best time in history, but I'm even more grateful for the friends who supported me through the writing process, including Pat Corrigan, Piers Bocock, Mary Flaherty, Dave Bacon, Doug Fishman, Zoë Bailey, Martha Kapur, Nancy Kaplan, Mary Lou Guthrie, Carol Schwartz, Jack Stenger, the Kirkwoods, Bill O'Brien, Andrew Sam, Jelena Kecmanovic, Fiona Macaulay, John Wimberly, Wes McCune, Kari Paludan, Drake Sorey, Mark Raabe, Vini Schoene, Emil de Cou, Beth Dolinger, Matt Gibson, and the ever-supportive SHRA fam, Eyrie brothers, Friends of Bill, New School colleagues, and JCPC community.

My family, especially my parents Joy Banton and Len Edwards, provided guidance, support and opportunities that helped me thrive and see the world in all its beauty and complexity. My sisters Stacie Woltman and Missy Pennington are an endless fount of love and support. Thanks to the loving community of my extended family: Roger Pennington, Julie Pennington, Shawn Pennington, Ken Woltman, Bill Banton, Tom Banton, Deb Banton, Al and Rosy Regni, Charlotte Lord, Alan and Maryann Thompson, Jesse Bouton, and the Brockways and McQuades.

Deep thanks to my University of Pennsylvania MAPP family for mentorship, learning, inspiration, and supportive community, especially my MAPP.12 siblings. Thank you, Marty Seligman, for creating positive psychology and building a science and a social movement that changed many lives (including mine). Special thanks to James Pawelski, Leona Brandwene, Aaron Boczkowski, Sidney Rubin, Laura Taylor, and Nicole Stottlemeyer for their help and inspiration at MAPP. Jer Clifton, Alejandro Adler, Emily Esfahani Smith, Cathrine Gyldensted, Allyson Mackey, Virginia Millar, Cory Muscara, Dan Tomasulo, and Judy Saltzburg helped me along the path in so many ways. Thank you!

It was great to work with Motivation Press and Author's Place. Thank you Justin Sachs, Tony Ferraro, Steve Lavey, and Teri Whitten, with a special shout out to Joseph Emnance for the outstanding cover he designed. Mike Mejer designed my wonderful website, Rob Jolles provided advice and guidance and connected me to my publisher, and Gina Hagler made my writing much better.

I am deeply grateful to Steven Pinker, Angela Duckworth, Dan Lerner, Dave Gardner, Gregg Easterbrook, Charles Kenny, and David Shenk for their help and encouragement. You all inspired me to tell the story about what is good in the world. I am also grateful to the late Hans Rosling, Max Roser, Steve Radelet, Robert Wright, Angus Deaton, Peter Diamandis, Steven Kotler, Johan Norberg, Matt Ridley, Marian Tupy, Ruth Defries, and Michael Shermer whose work inspired me and guided my path.

Most of all, my deepest gratitude goes to the two most important women in my life: Marissa Regni and Sofie Edwards. You make life better daily!

A NOTE ABOUT SOURCES

Thanks to the internet, it's very easy to find out about the good things, but you do need to look. When deciding on what important events from history to highlight, I often looked at the Wikipedia page for that day of the year. Other "This Day in History" websites, such as history.com, onthisday. com, and the Library of Congress' loc.gov/item/today-in-history, provided a start. I then researched the topics using a variety of resources, from Wikipedia to Encyclopedia Britannica. Since nearly all of the information and quotes in *The Daily Better* can be found in multiple sources, I only cited sources where specific information, such as recent statistics about education in India (June 1), was presented.

If you want to do your own research into the good things happening around the world, more and more high-quality sources are available. *Positive News* is a quarterly magazine that features stories about people solving problems and making the world a better place. *Gapminder* (gapminder.org) was founded by the late Hans Rosling. (His informative and very funny TED Talks are not to be missed.) *Gapminder* aggregates social and economic statistics on the user-friendly Gapminder Tools platform, which creates interactive visualizations depicting trends in income, mortality, education, and the like. *Human Progress* (humanprogress.org/) is both a data aggregator and blog about, you guessed it, human progress. On the website go to Your Life in Numbers (humanprogress.org/ylin), an interactive page where you plug in your vital statistics to see what your life would have been like in "the good old days." *Our World in Data*, led by Max Roser at Oxford, has a great website (ourworldindata.org) that provides dozens of charts, maps, and infographics that show how humans have made progress in many important ways.

There are also many excellent books. Here are my favorites:

- *The End of Doom: Environmental Renewal in the Twenty-first Century* by Ronald Bailey
- *The Big Ratchet: How Humanity Thrives in the Face of Natural Crisis* by Ruth Defries
- *It's Better Than It Looks: Reasons for Optimism in an Age of Fear* by Gregg Easterbrook
- *Abundance: The Future Is Better Than You Think* by Peter Diamandis and Steven Kotler
- *Getting Better: Why Global Development Is Succeeding--and How We Can Improve the World Even More* by Charles Kenny
- *Progress: Ten Reasons to Look Forward to the Future* by Johan Norberg
- *The Better Angels of Our Nature: Why Violence Has Declined* and *Enlightenment Now: The Case for Reason, Science, Humanism, and Progress*, both by Steven Pinker
- *Factfulness: Ten Reasons We're Wrong About the World--and Why Things Are Better Than You Think*, by Hans Rosling, Ola Rosling, and Anna Rosling Rönnlund
- *The Moral Arc: How Science Makes Us Better People* by Michael Shermer

- *The Optimism Gap: The I'm Ok-They're Not Syndrome and the Myth of American Decline* by David Whitman
- *Nonzero: The Logic of Human Destiny* by Robert Wright

I love discussing my work with students and readers. Reach out to me at henry@henryedwardsauthor.com and let's discuss pessimism, optimism, hope, and the future!

PREFACE

I magine a baby born in 1966. The child's mother visited the doctor regularly and followed his advice during her pregnancy. The baby boy took his first gulps of air in a hospital, attended by a doctor and nurses. He received excellent neonatal care. As he grew, he ate nutritious food and drank clean water. His parents brought him to the pediatrician for regular check-ups and vaccinations. Outside the home he attended elementary school because his parents didn't need to send him to field or factory to earn sustenance for the family. He even went on to secondary school. Fifty years later he's alive and in good health, having had no major medical problems in all 50 years since his birth.

Is this an extraordinary life? Today, billions would answer no. But they're wrong.

This child's life *is* extraordinary; the child is me. My life seems so ordinary because of incredible, unprecedented—and frequently overlooked—human progress. Before the mid-20th century, many children born to both paupers and princes died at rates that would shock us today. Until recently, most people did not get vaccinations. Today global vaccination rates top 80%, which means fewer and fewer of people die from infectious diseases. And nowadays more than 90% of children around the world attend some elementary school. This unprecedented progress means most children survive childhood, go to school, work productively for several decades, and grow old.

I was born during humanity's golden age, but, like nearly everyone else, I had no idea.

Like many postwar teens in America, I took my luck for granted. By the time I was in high school, I wasn't counting my blessings; I was obsessed with America's hypocrisy and the "evils" of capitalism. Beneath the surface of affluence, I imagined a rotten core of America—materialistic, militaristic, superficial, overweight...bloated both physically and metaphorically.

I also started believing that all of humanity was doomed for decline and fall. Like Chicken Littles in every previous generation, I thought that the end was near. I imagined we would all die from overpopulation or nuclear weapons. The TV news didn't help. Despite unparalleled progress, the news outlets dished out daily doses of war, terrorism, drugs, violence—humanity at its worst—in gory detail.

My psychology—depressed, anxious, cynical—mirrored my pessimistic worldview. In ninth grade I started using alcohol and drugs, and my high school partying slid into addiction. But thanks to my luck—living in these extraordinary times—finding help was easy. I got a therapist. I got sober. I got better.

In recovery from alcoholism, I was told to by mentors to develop "an attitude of gratitude." I was taught to appreciate my life and freedom from alcohol. The parents I ceaselessly complained about had, after all, kept me healthy and provided for me as I grew up. I had always been quick to see what's wrong with other people and the world as a whole, but I was slow to see what's right.

This attitude of gratitude, this daily attention to big and small gifts in my life, made me recognize my unfair prejudice against the world. Why did I think it was so screwed up?

My worldview started to shift. I began to see my life not as a suburban wasteland, but as a rich heartland of assets and opportunities. I stopped seeing America as irredeemably evil and started seeing its dark *and* bright sides, its atrocities in Vietnam and support of dictators, and its Marshall Plan and the Peace Corps. It made me think, "What other good things am I missing?"

I started asking different questions. What is the state of the world? Is there less poverty? Is the world more or less peaceful? In short, are we making progress?

I read dozens of books and, thanks to the modern miracle of the internet, I had unlimited information accessible at a keystroke. As I read more and talked to experts, I saw a pattern: the pessimists focused on the problems and stoked fears, but the optimists focused on the problems *and* the progress. It was the optimists who told the whole story.

As my worldview shifted, I felt my pessimism lifting. I became more optimistic, and I began to see all the things that are working in the world. I observed the vast infrastructure of modern life as connective, not alienating. I also made sure to see the sky, birds and mountains. I changed my view of humankind as parasites on the earth to intelligent animals that were learning from their mistakes. I was heartened by our success stories, how the once-burning Cuyahoga River in Cleveland is much cleaner today and home again to wildlife. I discovered that people from all over the earth had come together to make the world a better place. We were solving global problems like acid rain and the ozone hole.

We are working on ways to end global warming. Maybe there are reasons to be optimistic.

The more I learned, the more optimistic I became. As a child growing up in the 1970s, I feared three doomsday forces: communism, nuclear weapons, and overpopulation. The deadlock between East and West seemed perennial, and tensions increased when Reagan demanded that Gorbachev "tear down this wall." *The Day After* TV program brought a post-nuclear world to screens across America. Books like *The Population Bomb* prophesied massive famines. The future looked bleak.

But instead of getting worse, things got better. The fall of communism led to a massive reduction of nuclear weapons. We are no longer one international crisis away from Mutual Assured Destruction. Population growth has slowed, and the Green Revolution—contrary to the predictions of doomsayers—led to unparalleled food abundance, not famine.

I believe that the way forward is to examine the evidence and look at the broad picture of our world. We are very good at looking at the threats, thanks to the negativity bias, our very human tendency to pay more attention to what's bad. But we also need to look at what's good, what's working. By looking at the whole picture, we are more likely to solve our problems and avoid the pitfalls of pessimism.

And the big picture looks very bright. Literacy, education, longevity, technology, human rights, democracy and freedom have never been greater. Pestilence, War, Famine and Death—the Four Horsemen of the Biblical Apocalypse—are all in retreat.

I end by noting that there is a worldwide epidemic of anxiety, depression and suicide. The causes are many and complex, but I propose an additional cause: pessimism. Even though humanity is progressing rapidly on many fronts, people see the problems but not the progress. Many think that the world's been broken by humanity, and some even see us as unwelcome parasites on a miserable Mother Earth.

The Earth is not broken. It is a resilient planet that is home to *homo sapiens*, a species that has reached intelligence and consciousness of itself. We have produced the Pyramids and Angkor Wat, the Colosseum and the Forbidden City. We've composed *The Iliad* and *The Tale of Genji*, Beethoven's Ninth Symphony and the polyphonic songs of Pygmy Africans. We have been warlike but are now turning toward peace, democracy and human rights. And we are waking up to the damage we are doing to our home. We are healing the wounds and changing our relationship. From the creation of Yellowstone to the repair of the ozone hole via international cooperation, we have reasons to be optimistic. Global warming is our greatest current challenge, but we have a good track record when it comes to solving big problems. If we make a commitment to clean up our act, like we did for acid rain and the ozone hole, we can achieve the same success in the fight against climate change and make the world even better.

When I started seeing and appreciating the countless ways the world is getting better, I felt better. This is not Pollyanna-ism. I developed an accurate and balanced view of the world...*a realistic view that happens to be very inspiring!* I became an optimist because I saw, savored, and appreciated the good that is hidden in plain sight. The good that is not featured on the evening news.

THE DAILY BETTER gives you a once-a-day dose of what's good about the present. I hope you enjoy your daily dollop of optimism and share it with others.

INTRODUCTION

———

Try this on someone.

Go up to a friend and tell them how great things are. Say the world's never been better. Tell them that they should be optimistic about the future because the past 30 years have been the best, ever, and there's little reason to think that things will not continue to improve.

What will the response be?

I have asked this question to hundreds of people and the response is generally the same thing: *Are you kidding me?*

I am often accused of being naive or stupid or deluded. Rarely am I called clear-eyed or rational or fact-based. If I share the evidence about how good things are, the next response is "Yeah, but American politics are a mess" or "But what about terrorism?" Most people are very resistant to the idea that things are good and that the future is bright. Is the world going to hell?

No.

If our ancestors could see us today, they would be struck dumb by our good fortune. For 99% of our history, Nine out of ten of humans lived in extreme poverty, yet today that reality has been flipped: Less than 10% of the world lives in extreme poverty. Each day, economic growth in developing countries lifts 138,000 people out of poverty each day, according to author Johan Norberg. Killers like smallpox have been eradicated, and many other diseases that terrorized our grandparents' generation—polio, tuberculosis, measles—are in steep decline. Global life expectancy today is above 71 years, more than double what it was in 1800 (32 years), according to Max Roser at Oxford University. Most children—even girls in poor countries—go to elementary school, and four out of five humans can read. Interstate and civil wars, crime and violence are all near historic lows in many places. This short account of human progress is the tip of the iceberg. The good that's happening today and around the world could fill books and books.

So why do people think the world's going to hell?

One reason is the news. Switch on *CNN, Fox,* or the local station, and what do you see? Police on the scene of a terrorist attack. Distraught students interviewed in the wake of a school shooting. Disaster aftermath coverage showing flattened buildings and displaced people. Syria, Boko Haram, refugees, AK-47 toting youth, crime, political polarization. Is this what's happening? Does this reflect the state of the world?

The news media reports things that *happen.* Explosions and atrocities can be filmed; witnesses can be interviewed. There are real victims and real suffering. So it's understandable that the news reports distinct, usually negative, events. It's impossible to film or interview the 138,000 people who are lifted out of extreme poverty each day.

That said, how come there isn't more reporting of the good stuff?

The first reason is a human trait sculpted by evolution: the negativity bias, our tendency to pay more attention to threats and dangers. If our paleolithic ancestors had not paid attention to lions and snakes, they would have died. More important, they would not have reproduced (and you and I would not be here). The early humans who spotted dangers and felt fear survived. If you sit and smell the flowers on the African savanna, you're going to end up in some carnivore's belly.

Even though we no longer live among large predators, evolution has not removed our negativity bias. We pay attention to problems, threats and disasters, which is why we pay attention to the crime, war and disaster served up by the media.

A second trait of our psychology builds on the negativity bias. The availability heuristic is psychological terminology for our tendency to believe what we see. So if we watch "the news," which we think is "what's happening in the world," then we think that what's on the news is the state of the world. The news has always portrayed the explosive, scintillating and salacious, hence the trope "if it bleeds it leads." The news becomes a proxy for the state of the world. But the news does not reflect our better health and longer lives, our improving education and higher intelligence, our safe and peaceful world.

So what? The news may be negative, but is there any harm in it?

Yes. In two important ways.

First, the worldviews created by the news are inaccurate. Democracy requires an informed populace to make fact-based decisions about the candidates and issues. If the electorate's views of the world are skewed negative, the electorate will make negatively skewed decisions. Candidates who claim that crime is worse today than in the past are believed, despite a mountain of evidence that deems these times the safest ever. So instead of continuing effective policies that have led to the greatest crime decline ever, candidates who win on "crime is bad" platforms may be encouraged to implement policies that might undo the crime decline, such as mandatory sentences and brutal tactics.

Second, the negative news environment is bad for us.

Scientific studies demonstrate the negative psychological effects of negative news. Wendy Johnston and Graham Davey found that people exposed to negative news were sadder, more anxious, and obsessed more about their problems. In another study, Attila Szabo and Katey Hopkinson found "that watching the news on television triggers persisting negative psychological feelings that could not be buffered" easily. Another study, by Mary McNaughton-Cassill, found that exposure to the news was directly related to anxiety. In a 2014 poll conducted by National Public Radio, the Robert Wood Johnson Foundation, and the Harvard School of Public Health, a quarter of respondents said that the news was one of their biggest daily stressors.

How do we counteract the negative news machine that inaccurately portrays the world and makes us all feel worse? Daily doses of what's working. In short, *THE DAILY BETTER*.

This book contains 365 entries, one for each day of the year. In the morning, read and reflect on the theme of each day's story. You will learn about a person or an innovation from the past that makes today better and gives us reason to be optimistic about the future. Most entries highlight some good in modern life that did not exist in the past. Some entries describe an evil that is much less common today than it was in previous years. After each story is a "Thought for Today." For the rest of the day reflect on the hopeful theme and see what's working in the world.

THE DAILY BETTER will lift your mood and make you feel optimistic about our future. Spread it around every day!

JANUARY 1: THE MONTREAL PROTOCOL

The Montreal Protocol is the result of a process of scientific study, negotiations among the business and environmental communities, and international diplomacy.

~ Ronald Reagan ~

On this day in 1989, the Montreal Protocol came into force. It was a global agreement that stopped the use of chemicals contributing to ozone depletion. In the wake of the Protocol, ozone stabilized in the 1990s and then started to recover. Ozone levels are projected to return to pre-1980 levels by 2075.

In the 1980s and 90s, the hole in the ozone layer was considered by many to be an intractable problem, not unlike the present concerns about climate change. The Montreal Protocol demonstrated the potential of international agreements to solve global atmospheric problems.

THOUGHT FOR TODAY: In the recent past, governments and organizations have worked together to solve global environmental challenges like acid rain and the Antarctic ozone hole. The Montreal Protocol gives us hope that we can halt global climate change.

JANUARY 2: STARDUST

We are stardust, we are golden. We are billion-year-old carbon. And we got to get ourselves back to the garden.

~ Joni Mitchell ~

On January 2, 2004, the spacecraft *Stardust* swooped near the comet Wild 2 and collected material from its tail. *Stardust* sent these samples back to earth to be analyzed by scientists. Exploratory space missions like this were the stuff of science fiction not long ago, but nowadays space exploration is commonplace.

Humans have sent more than 4600 rockets into space. For virtually all of human history, space was seen as a faraway realm of heroes, gods and monsters. Now spacecraft connect the globe, predict the weather, and study the cosmos.

 **THOUGHT FOR TODAY:** Throughout the day, reflect on the wonders of space travel. If the sky is clear tonight, take time to look up and gaze at the beauty of the stars, planets...and satellites that streak across the night sky.

JANUARY 3: TOLKIEN'S MIDDLE EARTH

All that is gold does not glitter
Not all those who wander are lost

~ J.R.R. Tolkien ~

For millennia, humans have been telling stories. J.R.R. Tolkien, who was born this day in 1892, wrote tales of hobbits, elves and wizards that have been charming readers since *The Hobbit* was published in 1937. It is easy to dismiss these stories as kid's stuff, but heroic journeys still inspire both young and old. Joseph Campbell, a contemporary of Tolkien, popularized the power of myth in a book of that name. In good times and bad, stories allow us to dream, escape, and see our best selves depicted in the characters we meet.

THOUGHT FOR TODAY: What was your favorite story from childhood? Cast your mind back to the magical world conjured by the author. For the rest of the day, reflect on the bounty of stories we have to enjoy, be they short stories, novels or movies.

JANUARY 4: BRAILLE BRINGS READING TO THE BLIND

We do not need pity, nor do we need to be reminded that we are vulnerable. We must be treated as equals — and communication is the way we can bring this about.

~ Louis Braille ~

Blinded in a childhood accident, the brilliant Louis Braille created a tactile system of reading so revolutionary that it remains virtually unchanged to this day. Braille began a revolution in meeting the needs of the disabled that continues today. Technologies like braille, improved visual and hearing aids, and innovative prosthetics have made the life of the differently abled much better. And legislation like the Americans with Disabilities Act forced society to build a society for people of all abilities.

 **THOUGHT FOR TODAY:** Until recently, society made few concessions to people with diverse needs. Since Braille's time, the world has been changing to meet the needs of all people.

JANUARY 5: THE EIGHT HOUR WORKDAY

If you think you can do a thing or think you can't do a thing, you're right.

~ Henry Ford ~

A man works from sun to sun, but a woman's job is never done. In the "good old days" men worked 12 hours and women 18. Henry Ford doubled wages and introduced the eight-hour workday on January 5, 1914. This seemed like corporate suicide, but productivity increased after these changes and Ford's competitors followed suit. Today the eight-hour day is standard in most countries. And the modern innovation of two days off of work—the weekend—ushered in a new institution: leisure.

THOUGHT FOR TODAY: One hundred years ago, working hours and conditions in America were much worse. Labor unions, governments and industrialists like Henry Ford implemented reforms for safer, more humane working conditions, including the abolition of child labor.

JANUARY 6: MONTESSORI OPENS HER FIRST SCHOOL

Let the children be free; encourage them; let them run outside when it is raining.

~ Maria Montessori ~

The traditional classroom was designed like a factory where children were taught to sit in rows and follow orders. In her revolutionary approach to education, Maria Montessori allowed children to choose their activities and develop mastery based on the repetition of learning activities. Her success led to the widespread adoption of more progressive teaching pedagogies during the 20th century.

 **THOUGHT FOR TODAY:** Despite constant criticism of today's schools, education has never been better. Around the world, attendance and graduation rates are at all-time highs. Reflect on how much education has improved, especially in its commitment to individual learners and their personal thriving.

JANUARY 7: GALILEO SEES THE MOONS OF JUPITER

To understand the Universe, you must understand the language in which it is written, the language of mathematics.

~ Galileo Galilei ~

The 17th century was a time of scientific inquiry. Optical experimentation led to improved lenses and the development of spectacles, telescopes and microscopes. Gazing at Jupiter on the night of January 7, 1610, Galileo Galilei spied tiny dots of light near the great planet. By the next day he determined that he had discovered four moons of Jupiter. Galileo began a tradition of astronomy that has progressed far beyond his dim visions of Jovian moons 400 years ago.

THOUGHT FOR TODAY: Reflect on the inventions that have changed the way we see the world, from Galileo's first telescope to the Hubble telescope. Thanks to Galileo and thousands of inventors and astronomers that followed him, we are unraveling the mysteries of the cosmos.

JANUARY 8: LEONARDO'S *MONA LISA* IN THE UNITED STATES

Painting is a poetry that is seen rather than felt, and poetry is painting that is felt rather than seen.

~ Leonardo da Vinci ~

Once upon a time, only the rich and powerful could view artistic masterpieces. Michelangelo's *Pieta* or Raphael's *School of Athens* could only be seen by those who had access to the Vatican. Today it is an article of faith that the greatest artistic masterworks by humankind should be accessible to the public. On this day in 1963, da Vinci's *Mona Lisa* was displayed in the National Gallery in Washington, DC, a museum that costs nothing to visit. More than half a million visitors came to see it... for free.

THOUGHT FOR TODAY: Most of the humankind's masterworks, be they paintings, movies, writings, photography or sculpture, are available for people to visit or view virtually via the internet. Art is accessible for all people to view, savor and enjoy.

JANUARY 9: THE NIMROD EXPEDITION GETS CLOSE TO THE POLE

Men wanted for dangerous expedition: Low wages for long hours of arduous labour under brutal conditions.

~ Ernest Shackleton ~

On this day in 1909, Ernest Shackleton and his team of explorers were forced to abandon their trek to the South Pole due to treacherous conditions. Nonetheless, for two years his expedition would hold the record for getting closest to the Pole.

Shackleton was an inveterate Antarctic explorer whose most famous adventure happened five years later, the Imperial Trans-Antarctic Expedition. It failed miserably but became one of the greatest survival stories of all time. Despite being stranded on sea ice over an Antarctic winter and then rowing open lifeboats on the stormy Southern Ocean, all members of the expedition survived.

THOUGHT FOR TODAY: Reflect on bravery—both epic and everyday—that so many people possess. Whoever your heroes may be, they show us that anyone can perform courageous acts to explore, invent and make the world a better place.

JANUARY 10: SOME COMMON SENSE

A long habit of thinking a thing wrong, gives it a superficial appearance of being right. Time makes more converts than reason.

~ Thomas Paine ~

In early 1776, the 13 British colonies on the eastern coast of North America were in rebellion. In the previous year the war had started with the Battles of Lexington and Concord and Quebec City. On this day in 1776, Thomas Paine published *Common Sense*, a pamphlet that argued passionately, yet clearly and logically, for the 13 colonies to seek independence from Great Britain. It was an immediate sensation and remains one of the most popular writings in American history.

 **THOUGHT FOR TODAY:** Persuasive argument can bring about lasting positive change. This has been demonstrated many times in American history, from Common Sense through Uncle Tom's Cabin and To Kill a Mockingbird.

JANUARY 11: A WARNING FROM THE SURGEON GENERAL

A cigarette is a pipe with fire at one end and a fool at the other.

~ author unknown ~

On this day in 1964, the Surgeon General of the United States laid out the perils of tobacco in the report *Smoking and Health*. While this was not the first health warning about tobacco, it turned the tide against smoking in America. It led to laws that limited advertising, increased taxes, and mandated health warnings.

The decline of smoking has been a very positive trend in the last half century. Despite its once widespread appeal and highly addictive properties, smoking is seen for what it is—a killer—and young people are picking it up at much lower rates.

THOUGHT FOR TODAY: Public health programs, like anti-smoking campaigns, have led to better health and longer life. In 1964, 42% of Americans smoked. Today less than 17% do.

JANUARY 12: THE NATIONAL TRUST

A charity that works to preserve and protect historic places and spaces—for ever, for everyone.

~ The National Trust ~

Traditional philanthropy often means the endowment of museums, symphony orchestras and hospitals. In 1895 a new kind of philanthropy emerged: land bought for the sake of preservation and public enjoyment. On this day the National Trust was founded for these reasons. Today it is one of the largest charities in Great Britain. The National Trust owns hundreds of properties totaling nearly 1000 square miles.

THOUGHT FOR TODAY: Today nearly every community has parks both small and large for people to enjoy. Take time to appreciate the parklands in your community and around the world.

JANUARY 13: SLAVERY CONDEMNED!

Knowledge makes a man unfit to be a slave.

~ Frederick Douglass ~

O n this day in 1435—more than 50 years before Columbus set sail for the Americas—the Pope condemned the enslavement of the Guanche natives of the Canary Islands. Ironically, this would not stop the Europeans from enslaving Native Americans and Africans. Nonetheless, papal censure of enslavement was an important principle, one that would eventually become a universal principle.

THOUGHT FOR TODAY: Today slavery is illegal everywhere, but it is still practiced in some places. It is important to remember that for nearly all of human history, slavery was seen as a normal institution in society. Progress may seem slow, but one thread of the human story is the expansion of human rights.

JANUARY 14: ALBERT SCHWEITZER

Success is not the key to happiness. Happiness is the key to success. If you love what you are doing, you will be successful.

~ Albert Schweitzer ~

Albert Schweitzer was born on this day in 1875. A polymath, he distinguished himself both as a theologian and an organist. But he is best known for putting his faith into action by ministering to the sick in Gabon. With his wife, Dr. Schweitzer tirelessly worked in Africa fighting tropical disease and providing medical care where there was little modern medicine. For his work he received the Nobel Peace Prize in 1952.

THOUGHT FOR TODAY: The human race is peopled by many generous, dedicated people like Albert Schweitzer and Mother Theresa. We know from their experiences that humans have a well of kindness, generosity, and compassion that is celebrated too infrequently in the news.

JANUARY 15: A NEW KIND OF ENCYCLOPEDIA

Imagine a world in which every single person on the planet is given free access to the sum of all human knowledge. That's what we're doing.

~ Wikipedia founder Jimmy Wales ~

Diderot and the Encyclopédistes of the Enlightenment created the first comprehensive catalogue of human learning. *Encyclopedia Britannica* followed in 1768, and in the 1800s detailed reference resources flourished. By the mid-20th century, every middle-class home aspired to demonstrate a commitment to learning by showing off an encyclopedia in the living room or study.

Today we have *Wikipedia: The Free Encyclopedia*, which went online this day in 2001. Not only does it cost nothing; it's more accurate than many information sources because it is constantly updated by thousands of volunteers.

THOUGHT FOR TODAY: Today the poorest person in the world who is literate and has access to the internet has more information at her fingertips than presidents and prime ministers had just 20 years ago. The dissemination of learning and knowledge continues to accelerate.

JANUARY 16: RELIGIOUS FREEDOM GUARANTEED

All men shall be free to profess their opinions in matters of religion.

~ Virginia Statute for Religious Freedom ~

Until recent times, religious freedom was not guaranteed. At times the Romans were open to the many religions in their realm; at other times they persecuted Jews and Christians. Religious freedom as a human right is a new phenomenon in the long span of history. One important milestone was the Virginia Statute for Religious Freedom, authored by Thomas Jefferson and passed into law by the Virginia General Assembly on this day in 1786. It was a precursor to the guarantees enacted in the Bill of Rights several years later.

THOUGHT FOR TODAY: Religious freedom is an expectation in most of the world. For much of history, practicing a religion that was not officially sanctioned might bring a death sentence or expulsion. Today freedom of worship is an established right.

JANUARY 17: ANTARCTIC EXPLORATION

Ambition leads me not only farther than any other man has been before me, but as far as I think it possible for man to go.

~ James Cook ~

January is a busy time for Antarctic exploration. On this day in 1773, Captain James Cook was the first European, and possibly the first person, to sail south of the Antarctic Circle. A century and a half later, Roald Amundsen's expedition reached the South Pole. And instead of colonizing Antarctica, it is open to all nations. In the past, newly explored lands were chopped up between empires. According to the 1959 Antarctic Treaty, Antarctica may not be claimed by any country and is open to all for scientific exploration, a new notion in the history of human land exploration.

THOUGHT FOR TODAY: Exploration and daring-do seem to be in the blood of humans. Our desire to know more, explore, and experiment is one of our great traits.

JANUARY 18: A HOLIDAY FOR THE MAN WHO MADE AMERICA BETTER

Let us remember that the arc of the moral universe is long, but it bends toward justice.

~ Martin Luther King ~

In the 1980s and early 1990s, momentum grew to create a national holiday in honor of Martin Luther King. Despite Senator Jesse Helms' filibuster, the holiday became law in 1983.

More recently, President Barack Obama promoted making the holiday a "Day On." Nowadays, millions of Americans spend their MLK Day working on all kinds of service projects that make America better, just as King did in his brave opposition to racist laws.

THOUGHT FOR TODAY: Since the writing of the Declaration of Independence, Americans have fought to make the ideals of life, liberty and the pursuit of happiness real for all Americans. Thanks to the brave work of reformists, the circle of freedom continues to broaden, most recently to LGBT Americans. Heroes like Dr. King inspire us to make America better.

JANUARY 19: MAN OF STEEL

The good Lord made us all out of iron. Then he turns up the heat to forge some of us into steel.

~ Marie Osmond ~

Today is the birthday of Henry Bessemer, the English inventor who created a process for making steel from iron. It called for blasting air into iron to burn off impurities. Steel became better, cheaper, and more abundant. One of the many benefits of abundant, cheap steel was bridge safety. Iron bridges were much more prone to failure, but steel bridges could be built over longer spans with safer, more stable structures.

 **THOUGHT FOR TODAY:** It is easy to overlook the materials that undergird civilization, such as wood, aluminum, steel, plastic, and titanium. Yet they allow us to have more freedom to do more things. When you pass a skyscraper or a long suspension bridge, thank innovators like Bessemer for steel, the miracle metal that undergirds civilization.

JANUARY 20: PROTECTING LIBERTIES

Equal rights, fair play, justice, are all like the air: we all have it, or none of us has it.

~ Maya Angelou ~

On this day in 1920, the Civil Liberties Bureau became the American Civil Liberties Union (ACLU). Known today as a controversial organization that protects unpopular organizations, like the Ku Klux Klan and Nazi Party on the right, or the rights of defendants on death row. What cannot be disputed is they have been stalwart defenders of the civil rights guaranteed in the US Constitution.

THOUGHT FOR TODAY: Freedom is not free. Organizations of all stripes use the courts—and the court of public opinion—to guarantee that civil rights are upheld, even if they are unpopular. Such battles are the foundation of liberty.

JANUARY 21: A SERVICE ORGANIZATION IS FOUNDED

The best way to find yourself is to lose yourself in the service of others.

~ Mahatma Gandhi ~

The Supreme Lodge Benevolent Order Brothers was incorporated on this day in 1915. A year later, it changed its name to the Kiwanis, an Algonquin word meaning "to make oneself known." This service organization has focused its efforts on helping the children of the world. Today Kiwanians donate more than ten million hours of labor and one hundred million dollars each year.

THOUGHT FOR TODAY: Thousands of volunteer organizations around the world provide services to hundreds of millions of people in need. When your heart is broken by the bad news so often featured in the media, remember that the world is a good place filled with good people.

JANUARY 22: THE WARLIKE SWISS

The soldier above all others prays for peace, for it is the soldier who must suffer and bear the deepest wounds and scars of war.

~ Douglas MacArthur ~

Once upon a time, the Swiss were known as warriors. Their halberd and pikeman formations were formidable, and their soldiers were hired as mercenaries for warring European states. But over time, especially as wars became less frequent and soldiers were conscripted from the citizenry, Swiss mercenary services declined. Today the Swiss Guard, the defenders of the Vatican City, are a faint remainder of a warlike past. While the Swiss Army is very much a part of life in the Alps, it is best known for its multipurpose knives, not conquests.

THOUGHT FOR TODAY: Countries like Sweden, France and Switzerland were once famous for their warlike people. Today these countries are known as peaceful states. Though the news may make it seem like humans are in constant conflict, evidence suggests that wars are becoming less and less common.

JANUARY 23: MOTHER NATURE KILLS

Safety, in its widest sense, concerns the happiness, contentment and freedom of mankind.

~ William M. Jeffers ~

The Shaanxi earthquake struck on this day in 1556. It probably killed more than 800,000 people, making it the deadliest earthquake of all time.

One of the most underappreciated hallmarks of human progress is the decline in deaths from natural disasters. While we hear more news about natural disasters, the death and injury rates have declined significantly. As humans have improved building materials, methods, and codes, fewer people die in earthquakes and other disasters. Today, even though the population is nearly four times greater than it was in the 1920s, about 485,000 *fewer* people were killed in natural disasters each year, a rate decline of 32 times.

THOUGHT FOR TODAY: While natural disasters and their aftermath are reported in gory detail, the death and destruction have decreased sharply, thanks to human progress.

JANUARY 24: ATOMS FOR PEACE

Every gun that is made, every warship launched, every rocket fired signifies, in the final sense, a theft from those who hunger and are not fed.

~ Dwight Eisenhower ~

At the end of World War II, concerns about atomic weapons were high. While atom bombs ended the war, many wondered *Will they be used again?*

The first resolution of the United Nations created the Atomic Energy Commission on January 24, 1946. While the Commission's work stopped in the early 50s, President Eisenhower later promoted an "Atoms for Peace" agenda that led to the creation of the International Atomic Energy Agency (IAEA). The IAEA has played a major role in ensuring the nonproliferation of nuclear weapons.

THOUGHT FOR TODAY: Since Hiroshima and Nagasaki, people around the world have lived with the fear of nuclear war. Thanks to the IAEA, bilateral and multilateral treaties, and a commitment of nations to avoid nuclear war, no atomic weapons have been used since World War II.

JANUARY 25: SCHUSSING IN CHAMONIX

Citius, Altius, Fortius (faster, higher, stronger)

~ The Olympic Motto ~

The ancient games in Olympia involved racing, jumping, discus, javelin and other martial competitions in honor of Zeus. In 1896, the modern games revived the ancient tradition with an expanded palette of competitions with competitors throughout the world. During the second modern Olympics, women were included, and the 2012 games were the first ones in which all participating countries brought women contingents.

One of the most important milestones was the addition of the winter games, which debuted in Chamonix, France, on this day in 1924.

THOUGHT FOR TODAY: One hallmark of the modern world is trade, travel, and cooperation. Today we are drawn ever closer together by student exchanges, easy and cheap travel, tourism, and the Olympic Games.

JANUARY 26: THE APOLLO RELAUNCHES

In addition to the fans, I loved the feeling, the atmosphere, the spirit of the Apollo. The theater was history. It was the place for black entertainers. The big time.

~ Patti LaBelle ~

During 1920s and 30s, Harlem was the hippest section of Manhattan. On this day in 1934, the refurbished Apollo Theater reopened. It became the place "where stars are born and legends are made." The acts that played the Apollo were a veritable who's who of black musicians and acts. The audience reflected this mix of music styles and diversity.

The Apollo hit some hard times, especially in the 1970s, but today it is again the icon it was in its heyday. More than a million people visit the Apollo each year.

THOUGHT FOR TODAY: American music has been blessed with a cross-pollination of musical genres. The result is a rich and varied tapestry of styles. The Apollo Theater is an artistic institution that lives as a symbol American diversity.

JANUARY 27: THE WORLD GETS BRIGHTER

Our greatest weakness lies in giving up. The most certain way to succeed is always to try just one more time.

~ Thomas Edison ~

On this day in 1880, Thomas Edison patented the incandescent lamp. Before the age of electric light, illumination was expensive, dirty, and not very effective. Lighting at night required a flame of some kind, which gave off dirty smoke and created a fire hazard. In the 18th and 19th centuries, lighting improved with the development of kerosene lamps and gaslight, but it was the incandescent light bulb that illuminated the lives of millions.

THOUGHT FOR TODAY: With the development of cheap and ubiquitous electric light, Edison ushered in a new age. Today we can work and play whenever we want, and electric light has made our streets safer at night.

JANUARY 28: *PRIDE AND PREJUDICE* PUBLISHED

Give a girl an education and introduce her properly into the world, and ten to one she has the means of settling well, without further expense to anybody.

~ Jane Austen ~

On this day in 1813, Jane Austen's greatest work, *Pride and Prejudice*, was published. The romantic story of marriage for love or money speaks of the transition that was happening in the richest countries: People could marry for love, and not just for money. The rise of the novel also broadened the horizons of readers. Men who read Austen, Eliot or the Brontës realized that the interior worlds and aspirations of women were as rich as men's. Women who felt trapped by sexist institutions and customs saw a wider world, thanks to novels by women writers.

THOUGHT FOR TODAY: Until recent centuries, marriages were arranged for financial security, not love. Today most marriages are love marriages, and same-sex matrimony is becoming the norm, opening up life partnership to gay and straight people alike.

JANUARY 29: KARL BENZ PATENTS A NEW INVENTION

When Henry Ford made cheap, reliable cars people said, 'Nah, what's wrong with a horse?' That was a huge bet he made, and it worked.

~ Elon Musk ~

A famous (if apocryphal) saying of Henry Ford's is "If I had asked people what they wanted, they would have said faster horses." On this day in 1886, Karl Benz applied for a patent for his gasoline powered motorcar. His invention would change the world. Mobility, adventure and freedom were made easier as the automobile revolutionized life. Today the downsides of cars are salient, especially as contributors to greenhouse gases, but entrepreneurs like Elon Musk of Tesla are making electric cars that produce zero carbon emissions.

THOUGHT FOR TODAY: The automobile ended one of the worst forms of pollution: horse manure. City streets were once clogged with tons of feces. The innovation of the automobile ended horse pollution as a public health problem. Likewise, innovation in the 21st century is eliminating carbon emissions in cars.

JANUARY 30: A BRIDGE TO ANGLESEY

One mind can in a few hours think out enough work to keep a thousand men employed for years.

~ Washington Roebling ~

Ever since the first paleolithic human spanned a stream with a fallen log, people have used bridges to ease travel. Romans built arched aqueducts and bridges over rivers, such as the Pont du Gard in Nîmes, France. In recent centuries, iron, steel and suspension bridges spanned ever longer distances.

On this day in 1821, the Menai Suspension Bridge opened between the Welsh mainland to the Island of Anglesey. Washington Roebling built the Brooklyn Bridge in 1883, and even bigger bridges like the Golden Gate were constructed in the 1930s. Nine of the ten longest suspension bridges have been built since 1995, demonstrating that we continue to span formerly unbridgeable waterways.

 **THOUGHT FOR TODAY:** We build bridges to connect people, and in recent years our attempts have spanned new distances. We are more connected than ever.

JANUARY 31: REPEAL OF A DREADED LAW

The progress of freedom depends more upon the maintenance of peace, the spread of commerce, and the diffusion of education.

~ Richard Cobden ~

In the early 1800s, British peasants moved from farms to cities to work in factories. More food was needed to feed the urban working class. High tariffs against imported grains—known as the Corn Laws—meant food was expensive. This arrangement enriched aristocratic farmers, but it starved the working class.

The Anti-Corn Law League formed to oppose the dreaded laws. Led by Richard Cobdon, the League eventually prevailed upon Prime Minister Robert Peel to lead repeal efforts when the Irish potato crop failed. On this day in 1846, the Corn Laws were finally struck down.

THOUGHT FOR TODAY: The repeal of the Corn Laws was a blow against mercantilism and a boost for free trade. Today food and most goods are abundant and relatively inexpensive, thanks in part to free trade.

FEBRUARY 1: AN END AND A BEGINNING

An artist must be free to choose what he does, certainly, but he must also never be afraid to do what he might choose.

~ Langston Hughes ~

The joint resolution from Congress that became the 13th Amendment to the Constitution was signed this day in 1865. By the end of the year the requisite three-quarters of the states ratified the amendment, which ended slavery.

But slavery in lesser forms continued. Other February 1 milestones included the famous Greensboro, North Carolina, lunch counter sit in, one of many acts that pushed America toward full equality. And in 1998, Lillian E. Fishburne became the first female African American Rear Admiral in the Navy.

 **THOUGHT FOR TODAY:** Today we celebrate February as Black History Month. For most of American history, African Americans were treated as second-class citizens. While racism still exists, the arc of American history has slowly bent toward justice for black America.

FEBRUARY 2: SWAMPS BECOME WETLANDS

We have lost a sense of respect for the wild river, for the complex workings of a wetland, for the intricate web of life that water supports.

~ Sandra Postel ~

The word "swamp" has long been synonymous with dumping ground, rubbish heap, quagmire or morass. We now think of swamps as wetlands, places that filter and purify water, buffer floods, and stabilize the shoreline. The also provide critical habitat for wildlife.

On February 2, 1971, the Ramsar Convention was adopted. It provided mechanisms for international cooperation to protect wetlands. Since then, the contracting parties to the Convention meet regularly to implement, monitor, and enhance wetland programs. In honor of the good work done since the Ramsar Convention, February 2 is now celebrated as World Wetlands Day.

THOUGHT FOR TODAY: For much of history, humans drained and filled in swamps, which led to terrible environmental degradation. Today, nations cooperate closely to protect the land, sea, air and wetlands for a better planet and a better future.

FEBRUARY 3: A WIND OF CHANGE IN AFRICA

The construction of peace, progress and independence are hollow words unless they can be translated into a real improvement of living conditions.

~ Amilcar Cabral ~

Few empires give away the possessions they have stolen through deceit, realpolitik or outright invasion. This is true of ancient China, India, Persia, Arabia and medieval Europe. But on this date in 1960, Harold Macmillan, the conservative Prime Minister of Great Britain, hinted that decolonization of the UK's remaining colonies in Africa was going to happen. After this "Winds of Change" speech, all colonies except for Rhodesia (now Zimbabwe) and Namibia gained independence.

THOUGHT FOR TODAY: Domination of countries by foreign powers was once commonplace, but now it is unacceptable by international standards. Foreign dominion remains in a few places, such as China's rule of Tibet, but such colonization is a rare relic of the bad old days.

FEBRUARY 4: BIRTH OF A WARRIOR FOR WOMEN

Each suburban wife struggled with it alone. She was afraid to ask even of herself the silent question — "Is this all?"

~ Betty Friedan ~

On this day in 1921, Betty Friedan was born in Peoria, Illinois. After college, Friedan worked as a journalist until she was dismissed when she became pregnant with her second child. At her 15th college reunion, she surveyed fellow Smith College alumni and found that many of them felt squelched by society's expectations of women. Her book that grew from this project, *The Feminist Mystique*, was a catalyst for second wave feminism.

THOUGHT FOR TODAY: Nowadays women have reached nearly every level of power and influence in society. Inequalities remain, but girls today can hope to be mothers, authors, scientists...whatever they want, thanks to progress made by authors and activists like Betty Friedan.

FEBRUARY 5: BOBBY'S BOBBIES

The police are the public and the public are the police; the police being only members of the public who give full attention to duties in the interests of community welfare.

~ Robert Peel ~

Robert Peel was an important British politician, but his greatest legacy may be the "peelers" or "bobbies," the English police officers capped with the familiar police "custodian helmet." The Metropolitan Police of London were formed in 1829 by act of Parliament, and Robert Peel was a prime mover of this new professional public safety force that replaced a system of volunteers and low paid watchmen.

Peel, who was born this day in 1788, made his bobbies the first modern police force. Today professionally trained police keep law and order throughout the world, and professional policing is one reason why murder and violent crime rates are at or near historic lows.

 **THOUGHT FOR TODAY:** Modern, professional police forces are one of the many institutions that make the 21st century the safest time in human history.

FEBRUARY 6: CONCRETE ART BY MAILLART

Engineering is all about using the power of science to make life better for people, to reduce cost, to improve comfort, (and) to improve productivity.

~ N. R. Narayana Murthy ~

On this day in 1872, Swiss engineer Robert Maillart was born. He earned a traditional education in engineering, but Maillart chafed at the hyper-mathematical methods of his Swiss peers. He preferred to use intuition and common sense. This unconventional approach led to design breakthroughs and structurally innovative aesthetic masterpieces, like the Salginatobel and Schwandbach Bridges. His aesthetic sensibilities were so prized that his work was exhibited at the Museum of Modern Art in New York in 1947.

THOUGHT FOR TODAY: The science and beauty of modern architecture and engineering make our lives easier and more beautiful. For the rest of the day, take time to marvel at masterpieces of human engineering.

FEBRUARY 7: THE PLOW THAT BROKE THE PLAINS

Almost every year, in our long experience, we have discovered and applied some new feature to our plows, enhancing their value.

~ John Deere ~

John Deere's humble beginnings in Rutland, Vermont did little to foreshadow his groundbreaking impact on agriculture. In Vermont he apprenticed to a blacksmith and later took his skills to the prairies of Illinois. There he noted that the iron plows did a poor job of turning over the clay soils of the prairie, so he designed a steel plow and refined the shape of the moldboard. His improved plow sold like hotcakes, and Deere's invention became known as "the plow that broke the plains."

THOUGHT FOR TODAY: John Deere's company continues today, and the innovations at Deere and hundreds of other companies mean that farmers produce more food than ever. Despite an increasing world population, we produce more food per capita than ever.

FEBRUARY 8: A STANDARD TIME FOR A UNIFIED WORLD

If you love life, don't waste time, for time is what life is made up of.

~ Bruce Lee ~

On this day in 1879, Canadian engineer Sandford Fleming first proposed a global standard time. This idea germinated three years earlier when he missed a train in Ireland because of an error on the printed schedule. Fleming suggested dividing the world into 24 time zones, each approximately 15 degrees of longitude in width. He also suggested a 24-hour clock instead of two cycles of 12 hours each day. His principles were adopted and are still in force today.

THOUGHT FOR TODAY: Over time, innovators and organizations have found ways to integrate the world into ever more coordinated systems of cooperation. This has pulled people and nations closer together in mutual benefit and peaceful commerce.

FEBRUARY 9: UNITED STATES WEATHER BUREAU ESTABLISHED

Sunshine is delicious, rain is refreshing, wind braces us up, snow is exhilarating; there is really no such thing as bad weather, only different kinds of good weather.

~ John Ruskin ~

Predicting the weather has traditionally been a dodgy prospect. On this day in 1870, President Ulysses S. Grant signed the resolution that created the United States Weather Bureau. At that time prediction was still crude, but the telegraph—first used in 1844—allowed the exchange of observations as weather made its way west to east across America.

Today complex weather modeling computer programs that crunch millions of atmospheric data points have made weather prediction much more accurate. And anyone with a smartphone or computer can watch real-time radar as weather formations come and go.

THOUGHT FOR TODAY: The science of meteorology, while still imperfect, has advanced to such a point that storm prediction saves thousands of lives each year, and everyday people can plan travel, work, and leisure around the weather.

FEBRUARY 10: THE COMFORT OF SEX

When I'm good, I'm very good, but when I'm bad, I'm better.

~ Mae West ~

Sexuality has rarely been celebrated in human history. While ancient treatises like the Kama Sutra exist, most religions have seen desire as a source of suffering (Buddhism) or as a potentially sinful diversion (Christianity and Islam). It is no surprise that as women gained rights during the 1960s, notably access to birth control pills, exploration of the pleasures of sex became more public and important.

Today is the birthday of Alex Comfort, author of *The Joy of Sex*. The title—a puckish play on a popular middlebrow cookbook *The Joy of Cooking*—extolled the endless variations and simple recipes to make sex more adventurous and exciting.

THOUGHT FOR TODAY: Today sexual pleasure is considered a laudable goal in its own right, not a sign of sensual sin. Take time to enjoy the freedoms—and comforts—of sex.

FEBRUARY 11: FREE NELSON MANDELA!

It is better to lead from behind and to put others in front. You take the front line when there is danger. Then people will appreciate your leadership.

~ Nelson Mandela ~

On this day in 1990, Nelson Mandela was released from prison after more than 27 years of confinement. After his release he promised to work toward peace and reconciliation with the white minority government. Eventually elections were held and a coalition government transitioned the country from white minority rule to true democracy. Mandela was elected president in 1994. He and F.W. de Klerk were awarded the Nobel Peace Prize for their work in ending apartheid and creating a fully democratic South Africa.

THOUGHT FOR TODAY: One hundred years ago, European countries and colonists ruled virtually all of Africa. In recent times, white minority governments in Rhodesia (Zimbabwe) and South Africa have ceded their monopolies on power. Today there are more than 20 democracies in Africa.

FEBRUARY 12: THE NAACP IS ESTABLISHED

What a world this will be when human possibilities are freed, when we discover each other, when the stranger is no longer the potential criminal and the certain inferior!

~ W.E.B. Du Bois ~

On this day in 1909, W.E.B. Du Bois, Mary White Ovington, and Moorfield Storey founded the NAACP. The civil rights organization's goal was to secure equal rights for all people "and to eliminate race-based discrimination." The organization was at the forefront of the civil rights movements throughout the 20th century and continues its work today. NAACP attorneys often led fights in the court to advance the cause of equality. One of its most famous attorneys, Thurgood Marshall, eventually became the first African American justice of the Supreme Court.

THOUGHT FOR TODAY: The NAACP, like many citizen-founded groups, has successfully fought to force America to live up to its ideals. In recent years, similar citizen groups have successfully advocated for equal rights regardless of sexual orientation and identification, sex, and cognitive ability.

FEBRUARY 13: THE BISON HUNT RESUMES

What is life? It is the flash of a firefly in the night. It is the breath of a buffalo in the winter time. It is the little shadow which runs across the grass.

~ Crowfoot ~

With the encouragement of the US government, bison were nearly hunted to extinction in the late 1800s. Since then, the population has slowly climbed back. Today there are approximately 500,000 bison in America, 30,000 of which are considered wild.

On this day in 2011, Indian tribes that were guaranteed by treaties to hunt buffalo did so for the first time in more than 100 years. While the hunts have proved controversial for some, the Native Americans for whom the bison hunt is a part of their ancient culture, this is a welcome renewal.

THOUGHT FOR TODAY: European and American settlers wrecked death and destruction upon Indians and wildlife. Today, efforts are being made to restore once near-extinct animals and repair relationships with Native Americans.

FEBRUARY 14: FREDERICK DOUGLASS

It is easier to build strong children than to repair broken men.

~ Frederick Douglass ~

Despite growing up an enslaved man, Frederick Douglass became one of America's most brilliant minds. He secretly learned how to read and write, something his "master" feared lest Douglass want to seek his freedom. Seek it he did. He escaped North and became an author, speaker and leader of the abolitionist movement.

For most of human history, slavery was a "normal" part of society. Yet today every country outlaws it. Slavery is still common in some countries, like Mauritania and Uzbekistan, but it is illegal nonetheless.

THOUGHT FOR TODAY: While slavery remains a problem, no country allows it legally, and nations and NGOs fight hard to stamp out what remains of the ancient practice. The demise of slavery is one of humankind's many great achievements.

FEBRUARY 15: SUSAN B. ANTHONY

It was we, the people; not we, the white male citizens; nor yet we, the male citizens; but we, the whole people, who formed the Union.

~ Susan B. Anthony ~

Susan B. Anthony, born on this day in 1820, was a tireless reformer. She began her career as an abolitionist and then worked in the temperance movement. Anthony then turned to women's rights, for which she earned enduring fame. Anthony was famously arrested in 1872 for voting. She died in 1906, but 14 years later, the 19th Amendment to the US Constitution was ratified, giving women the right to vote in national elections.

THOUGHT FOR TODAY: Until recently women had few legal rights and were treated as the property of men. The tireless work of suffragists like Anthony opened the vote to females, and the number of women in elected office continues to climb around the world.

FEBRUARY 16: SUPERCENTENARIANS

Eat your vegetables, have a positive outlook, be kind to people, and smile.

~ Kamada Nakasato, a 102-year-old Okinawan,
on how to live a long life ~

When Eugénie Blanchard was born in 1896, the world average life expectancy was about 30 years. This number was low in part because child mortality rates were very high. Today the world average life expectancy is approximately 70 years. Nowadays supercentenarians—people who live past 110—are becoming more and more common. Eugénie Blanchard lived to 114 years, and longevity records continue to be broken. Some doctors and scientists have predicted an upper limit to the length of human life, but that "limit" keeps getting pushed higher and higher with no end in sight.

THOUGHT FOR TODAY: In the last century, life expectancy has doubled. Unlike thousands of previous generations, we can expect to live long, healthy lives full of opportunities for education, abundant and varied food, good health care, and opportunities to pursue our dreams.

FEBRUARY 17: A FRENCH COMEDIAN'S LEGACY

(Molière) has been accused of not having a consistent style, but they are trifles in comparison to the wealth of character he portrayed and his technique.

~ Martha Bellinger ~

The French comedic playwright Molière died on this day in 1673. Famous for such plays as *The Misanthrope, Tartuffe,* and *The Bourgeois Gentleman,* Molière relished making fun of doctors, hypocrites and misers. His pointed observations of French high society of the Age of Louis XIV often hit close to home, earning him animosity as well as high praise.

THOUGHT FOR TODAY: Nowadays, excellent comedy is ubiquitous, be it in clubs, on cable channels, or in writing. Comedy and satire deflate the bloated egos of leaders, make us laugh, and help us keep perspective. Take time today to enjoy comedy, be it Saturday Night Live reruns or live stand-up.

FEBRUARY 18: AIR MAIL TAKES OFF

The Net is not television. It is direct mail with free stamps, and it allows you to create richer and deeper relationships than you've ever been able to create before.

~ Seth Godin ~

The first mail delivery delivered via airplane happened on this day in 1911. It was dreamed up as fundraising scheme by two men, one of whom was Walter Windham, who would later initiate airmail service in the UK. Windham piloted the plane that carried 6500 pieces of mail a few miles from an airfield north of Delhi, India to a nearby town.

In the 21st century, millions of parcels and letters are delivered via airmail each day. Speedy and relatively inexpensive national and international mail is a part of contemporary life.

THOUGHT FOR TODAY: Nearly anything we want or need can be sent anywhere in the world for a reasonable price. We are knit together in a complex web of communication, trade and exchange.

FEBRUARY 19: A CHANGING VIEW OF THE UNIVERSE

To know that we know what we know, and to know that we do not know what we do not know, that is true knowledge.

~ *Nicolaus Copernicus* ~

For 1500 years, Claudius Ptolemy's treatise on astronomy, *Almagast*, was considered the last word on astronomy. But Renaissance scholars challenged the Ptolemaic understanding of the universe. Nicolaus Copernicus, while studying law at Bologna, befriended astronomer Domenico Maria Novara and exchanged observations and ideas about the cosmos. This fruitful friendship may have led to Copernicus' shifting thinking about the motion of the heavenly bodies. Copernicus argued that the earth and planets orbited the sun, which contradicted Ptolemy's views that the earth was the center of the universe.

THOUGHT FOR TODAY: Scientific revolutions rock our worldviews, but the progression of science leads toward more accurate understandings of the universe. These understandings lead to breakthroughs in medicine, agriculture and other practical sciences that decrease human suffering, increase well-being...or just help us to understand our fascinating universe.

FEBRUARY 20: JOHN GLENN ORBITS THE EARTH

If there is one thing I've learned in my years on this planet, it's that the happiest and most fulfilled people I've known are those devoted to something bigger.

~ John Glenn ~

On this day in 1962, astronaut John Glenn became the first American to orbit the Earth aboard the *Friendship 7* Mercury capsule. He was not the first, as Soviet cosmonaut Yuri Gagarin was both the first person in space and the first person to orbit the planet. America was trailing in the space race, so Glenn's flight and three orbits were a needed boost for the NASA program.

 **THOUGHT FOR TODAY:** Two generations ago there was no space travel. Today humanity maintains a constant presence in space, and plans are underway for travel to Mars. For the rest of the day, ponder the wonder of space travel, which has broadened our understanding of the cosmos and opened new frontiers for humanity.

FEBRUARY 21: DEBUT OF A LITERARY INSTITUTION

Think as you work, for in the final analysis, your worth to your company comes not only in solving problems, but also in anticipating them.

~ Harold Ross ~

On this day in 1925, *The New Yorker* magazine debuted. It featured the works of many of the most prominent American authors, notably Truman Capote, Dorothy Parker and John Updike. Many bemoan the supposed decline in American prose, but every generation has made this same prediction, and *The New Yorker* continues lives on at the apex of the American literary universe.

 **THOUGHT FOR TODAY:** In 1925, when The New Yorker debuted, approximately one-third of the world was literate. Today four-fifths of the planet are can read. In the US and around the world, average IQ scores have increased more than 25 points since the 1920s. Despite the moaning of the older generation about the demise of spelling and handwriting, the kids today are more literate than any previous generation.

FEBRUARY 22: A PEOPLE POWER REVOLUTION IN THE PHILIPPINES

I don't have any formula for ousting a dictator or building democracy. All I can suggest is to forget about yourself and just think of your people.

~ Corazon Aquino ~

At about 6:30 p.m. on this day in 1986, Philippines Defense Minister Juan Ponce Enrile and General Fidel Ramos held a press conference at Camp Aguinaldo, where they announced that they were withdrawing support from Ferdinand Marcos' government. Within days, Marcos' corrupt government would be overthrown, and elections would sweep Corazon Aquino into the presidency.

The Philippine People Power revolution influenced popular revolts against dictatorships in South Korean, Burma, China and Indonesia. Even Václav Havel said that People Power inspired the Velvet Revolution he led in the Czech Republic.

THOUGHT FOR TODAY: When you cast a vote or hear the news of an election in another country, remember that democracy has only become commonplace since World War II and especially since 1990. Though progress has been uneven, democracy continues to spread in the 21st century.

FEBRUARY 23: THE FIRST BESTSELLER

It is a press from which shall flow in inexhaustible streams, the most abundant and most marvelous liquor that has ever flowed to relieve the thirst of men!

~ Johannes Gutenberg ~

Few innovations changed the world the way Gutenberg's printing press did. His most important publication was the *Bible*. It is believed that his famed Gutenberg *Bible* went on sale this day in 1455.

Gutenberg's revolution led to the widespread availability of books and an increase in literacy. The Reformation, which would start in the early 1500s, emphasized literacy so that Christians could read the *Bible*. As individual Christians, not religious authorities, began to read and interpret the *Bible*, individualism increased.

THOUGHT FOR TODAY: When you pick up a book, remember that books were rare and expensive in the past. Only the rich and powerful owned books and learned how to read. Before Gutenberg's time, only a tiny percentage of citizens could read. Today more than 85% of the world population is literate, and rates continue to rise.

FEBRUARY 24: TIME IS PRECIOUS

Your time is limited, so don't waste it living someone else's life. Don't be trapped by dogma - which is living with the results of other people's thinking.

~ Steve Jobs ~

Accurate timekeeping has fueled progress. Time is the one non-renewable resource, so more efficient measurement and management of time has been key to human advancement.

On this day in 1582, the Pope promulgated *Inter gravissimas*, which made the new Gregorian calendar official. The new calendar was in sync with the seasonal year, which made it more user friendly for farmers and townspeople alike.

THOUGHT FOR TODAY: Some people bemoan our society's sometimes slavish obsession with time, but this value reflects how precious time is. By accurately measuring and managing our time, we are able to use this non-renewable source better.

FEBRUARY 25: THE WARSAW PACT ENDS IN PEACE

From Stettin in the Baltic to Trieste in the Adriatic an iron curtain has descended across the Continent.

~ Winston Churchill ~

East versus West, Communism versus Capitalism, USSR versus US. For more than 40 years after the end of World War II, much of humanity was locked in a bipolar world of NATO versus the Warsaw Pact. Each alliance sat to the east or west of a line that came to be known as the Iron Curtain.

On this day in 1991, the six remaining members of the Warsaw Pact disbanded the alliance. This was another milestone in the pacification of Europe, a peace that remains today.

THOUGHT FOR TODAY: Much of European history is a confusing tangle of wars and conflicts. Today a war between European powers is hard to imagine. We live in the most peaceful time in human history, and as trade, travel, and communications increase, major wars become less and less likely.

FEBRUARY 26: RADAR

There is a great deal of satisfaction in the elegant demonstration that the theory is not quite right and has to be worked over again, very much as any other work of art.

~ Robert Watson-Watt ~

In the 1920s and 30s, radio waves crackled around the world, delivering entertainment and news to grateful humans. Meantime, scientists pondered other uses of these waves. On this day in 1935, British scientists Robert Watson-Watt and Arnold Wilkins made the first demonstration of radar technology for tracking aircraft. It was fortunate for the Brits that this breakthrough happened before war with Germany commenced in 1939, for during the Battle of Britain, radar saved the nation from Luftwaffe air superiority and therefore prevented a German invasion.

THOUGHT FOR TODAY: Today radar helps us to fly safely, track weather, and catch speeding drivers. Radar, like so many other technologies developed in the 20th century, makes our life safer and better.

FEBRUARY 27: BIRTH OF A CONSUMER CRUSADER

When strangers start acting like neighbors communities are reinvigorated.

~ Ralph Nader ~

Today marks the birthday of consumer crusader Ralph Nader. He studied law at Harvard, where he wrote his first published critique of the American automotive industry. In the mid-60s he wrote his breakthrough book, *Unsafe at Any Speed*, which pointedly criticized the GM Corvair. His activism moved beyond autos when he expanded his work to food safety, insecticides and coal mine safety. He founded public interest organizations like the Center for Responsive Law and Public Citizen. He even ran for president several times on the Green Party ticket.

THOUGHT FOR TODAY: While controversial, Nader popularized modern consumer advocacy. Today a bevy of consumer product organizations work to ensure the safety of what is manufactured and advocate for business practices that benefit society. Thanks to their work, consumer products are safer than ever.

FEBRUARY 28: CAROTHERS CREATES NYLON

In his research, Carothers was never content to follow the beaten path or to accept the usual interpretations of organic reactions.

~ James B. Conant ~

Wool, silk linen and a few other varieties of thread clothed humans for most of recorded history. But in modern times, as scientific understanding of chemistry progressed, many new materials were invented. One of the most important was nylon, which was created on this day in 1935. Carothers was a brilliant scientist who made many breakthrough discoveries, including polyesters and neoprene, in addition to nylon. Nylon was developed more than 80 years ago, yet it still is widely used due to its strength, elasticity, abundance and low price.

THOUGHT FOR TODAY: Synthetic fibers often get a bad rap, but they are used for items both mundane (stockings) and lifesaving (parachutes). For most of history, people had but one or two sets of clothing. Today, thanks in part to manmade fibers, clothing is abundant, inexpensive and high quality.

MARCH 1: AMERICA'S BEST IDEA

There is nothing so American as our national parks. The fundamental idea behind the parks is that the country belongs to the people.

~ Theodore Roosevelt ~

In 1871, the Hayden Expedition explored parts of the American West and returned to Washington with detailed reports about the land, including its flora and fauna. Most importantly, photographer William Henry Jackson and painter Thomas Moran captured the visual beauty of the region, notably the geothermal features in northwest Wyoming. The report and pictures convinced Congress to set aside the land, which established Yellowstone National Park.

The Act of Dedication that created Yellowstone became a template for the US National Park System. Today there are 58 National Parks and a total of 417 National Park Sites.

THOUGHT FOR TODAY: Around the world there are more than a thousand national parks. Little did the men of the Hayden Expedition know that they planted the seed that would become "America's Best Idea."

MARCH 2: HIGH QUALITY SCHOOLING FOR ALL, REGARDLESS OF ABILITY

The only thing worse than being blind is having sight but no vision.

~ Helen Keller ~

The first school for the blind in the United States was founded on this day in 1829. John Dix Fisher was inspired to create the school after visits to the National Institute for the Blind in Paris. The school was named for Thomas Perkins, one of the school's incorporators and a Boston merchant whose sight was failing at the time. Today hundreds of schools for the blind exist around the world.

THOUGHT FOR TODAY: In ancient times, blind babies were sometimes left to die or sold into slavery as prostitutes. Over time, compassion toward people with disabilities increased, as did support, education and protections. Today blindness is often curable, thanks to advances in medicine.

MARCH 3: ANNE SULLIVAN BEGINS HER WORK

Each time you fail, start all over again, and you will grow stronger until you have accomplished a purpose.

~ Anne Sullivan ~

Anne Sullivan grew up as a poor child of immigrants. She was visually impaired and went to the Perkins School for the Blind (see March 2). Her first job out of Perkins was to teach Helen Keller, a blind and deaf girl from a well-to-do family in Alabama. Upon her arrival, Sullivan bickered with the Kellers, but her commitment to Helen and success teaching her endeared Sullivan to the family. Eventually Sullivan took Helen to Perkins, and the young Keller became the brightest star of the school. Keller became a symbol of the potential and possibilities of the disabled.

THOUGHT FOR TODAY: Keller was the first blind person to earn a college degree in America. Today millions of blind people are fluent in braille and sign language, and thousands of visually impaired students graduate from college each year.

MARCH 4: PROTECTION FOR THE COMMON LABORER

The purpose of the Department of Labor shall be to foster, promote and develop the welfare of working people.

~ 29 U.S. Code § 551 ~

On this day in 1913, The US Department of Labor was created when president William Howard Taft reluctantly signed it into law. The Department of Labor was established to implement and monitor worker safety regulations, wage and working conditions standards, unemployment benefits, employment services for job seekers, and the tallying of labor statistics.

Over the course of the 20th century, the American labor force would grow to create the greatest industrial power of all time. With that growth came higher wages, better housing, educational opportunities, and spreading prosperity.

THOUGHT FOR TODAY: When the Labor Department was formed, there were few protections for laborers, but as the 20th century progressed, organizations like the Department of Labor established guidelines and protections to improve the well-being of blue-collar Americans.

MARCH 5: A PORTENTOUS SPEECH IN FULTON, MISSOURI

You have enemies? Good. That means you've stood up for something, sometime in your life.

~ Winston Churchill ~

From Stettin in the Baltic to Trieste in the Adriatic, an iron curtain has descended across the continent. Theses ominous words, delivered by Winston Churchill on this day in 1946, correctly observed that the world was freezing into two warring blocs, Eastern Communism versus Western Democracy. The Cold War continued for another 40 years.

But in the 1980s the Cold War thawed when President Reagan and Premier Gorbachev begin the process that led to the end of the East-West divide.

 **THOUGHT FOR TODAY:** It is easy to forget that we live in a unique era: There are no major power struggles between major powers. By the end of the Cold War, humanity's better angels prevailed and nuclear war between East and West was averted.

MARCH 6: MICHAELANGELO

The greatest danger for most of us is not that our aim is too high and we miss it, but that it is too low and we reach it.

~ *Michelangelo Buonarroti* ~

Michelangelo once said "The true work of art is but a shadow of the divine perfection." But when one is in the presence of his *Pieta, David* or the Sistine Chapel, it seems the great artist got pretty close. He was born on this day in 1475 and, like many of his Italian contemporaries, he pushed artistic achievements to celestial heights.

He achieved those heights on the Sistine Chapel ceiling. It was difficult to reach—he built an elaborate scaffolding—and was not designed for frescoes. But from this difficult canvas he created a work of divinity about divinity.

THOUGHT FOR TODAY: The perfections created by artists like Michelangelo, Vermeer and Georgia O'Keeffe remind us that life is beautiful, the world is stunning, and humanity is capable of creating exquisite beauty.

MARCH 7: A DAY OF REST

I have never in my life found myself in a situation where I've stopped work and said, "Thank God it's Friday." But weekends are special.

~ Helen Mirren ~

On this day in 321, Roman Emperor Constantine declared that *dies Solis Inviciti* (Sun-day) would be henceforth the day of rest. Constantine's declaration forms the basis of our Sunday, the one day of rest.

Two days of rest—the weekend—started in the late 1800s in England where workers were allowed to leave work at 2pm on Saturday. In the early 1900s, some US mills in New England shuttered factories so Jewish workers could take their sabbath on Saturday. Henry Ford's decision to give workers a five-day week was also influential.

 **THOUGHT FOR TODAY:** Over the course of history, humans have gained more leisure time. The weekend is a relatively recent innovation, and many countries and locales are experimenting with a four-day work week. If past is prologue, then the three-day weekend may be coming.

MARCH 8: WALL STREET BEARS AND BULLS

Because of the love affair between the American public and the stock market, it is possible for entrepreneurs, technological visionaries and inventors to get financing.

~ Ron Chernow ~

The New York Stock Exchange (NYSE) is the world's largest stock exchange, and hundreds of billions of dollars can change hands each day. It was founded on this day in 1817. The growth of NYSE paralleled the economic growth of the United States. As wealth grew, more and more Americans bought stock and benefited from the rapid rise of American business. With each financial panic or crash, reforms were demanded that forced companies to operate with greater transparency.

THOUGHT FOR TODAY: In the 21st century more than half of Americans own some kind of stock. For most of history, the poor constituted the largest class of society, but in recent centuries, the middle class has grown to become the largest and most important class, thanks in part to the wealth-spreading effects of widespread stock ownership.

MARCH 9: THE AMISTAD DECISION

> What can be more false and heartless than this doctrine which makes the first and holiest rights of humanity to depend upon the color of the skin?
>
> ~ *John Quincy Adams* ~

The enslavement of Africans is one of the worst blights on the conscience of America. Sometimes the United States did the right thing, and one was the case of *The Amistad*. A group of kidnapped Africans revolted on their ship and took it over, but they were eventually intercepted by a US vessel. President Van Buren planned to return the kidnapped Africans to them. The case went to the Supreme Court, and the Africans were represented by John Quincy Adams. The high court ruled in favor of the Africans.

THOUGHT FOR TODAY: The Amistad decision did little to end slavery, but it was a boost to the abolitionist movement. Moral progress is slow but it marches nonetheless. As Martin Luther King said, "the arc of the moral universe is long, but it bends toward justice."

MARCH 10: WATSON, COME HERE...

When one door closes, another opens; but we often look so long and so regretfully upon the closed door that we do not see the one which has opened for us.

~ Alexander Graham Bell ~

There are billions of telephones in the world today, so it is hard for us to imagine a world without them. They didn't exist 150 years ago. In the mid-1800s, telegraphs were the only technology for sending long-range messages. Many scientists worked to invent a voice transmission technology. One of these scientists, Alexander Graham Bell, was the first to create and successfully test a two-way voice transmission device.

On this day in 1876, Bell uttered these famous words to his assistant: "Watson, come here, I want to see you!" The rest is telephonic history.

THOUGHT FOR TODAY: Every few years new breakthroughs make communication easier and easier. The ongoing cascade of technological progress undoes isolation and draws people together from all parts of the world.

MARCH 11: COAL FUELS THE INDUSTRIAL REVOLUTION

The clear and present danger of climate change means we cannot burn our way to prosperity. We need a clean industrial revolution.

~ Ban Ki-moon ~

Great Britain has been very fortunate. A European power, it was protected from invasion by the English Channel. In the 1800s, Britons discovered that their country was blessed with copious coal seams that would fuel the industrial revolution.

One of Britain's many collieries—the Seven Sisters mines in South Wales—began operations on this day in 1872. It provided high quality anthracite to feed the furnaces of industry in Wales and England.

THOUGHT FOR TODAY: Global warming is the world's biggest environmental threat, but we can take heart that over the course of the industrial revolution, humanity has turned to cleaner and cleaner fuels. Dirty coal gave way to cleaner petroleum and natural gas. Now zero-carbon sources such as nuclear power, solar, wind and geothermal are replacing carbon.

MARCH 12: A GREAT MARCH BEGINS

First they ignore you, then they laugh at you, then they fight you, then you win.

~ Mohandas Gandhi ~

For most of human history, protests were crushed by kings and emperors. Peaceful protest became a powerful tool in the 19th and 20th century. One of the great peaceful protesters of all time, Mohandas Gandhi, began an important protest on this day in 1930. The Salt March was an act of tax resistance against the British colonial government, who had outlawed traditional forms of salt collection.

This act of nonviolent civil disobedience galvanized Indian and world opinion against the British and gave a strong boost to the Indian self-rule movement.

THOUGHT FOR TODAY: Protest is part and parcel of progress. Gandhi was inspired by previous acts of nonviolent disobedience, like protests by American women suffragists. Many reform movements achieved their aims by using nonviolent methods to change the world for the better.

MARCH 13: THE FAR PLANETS DISCOVERED

Coelorum perrupit claustra (He broke through the barriers of the heavens.)

~ Epitaph at grave of William Herschel ~

Ancient humans weren't sure what to make of the night sky, except to gasp in awe at its beauty. Ptolemy created a complex system to explain the movement of the celestial bodies and placed the earth at the center of the universe. Galileo, Copernicus and Kepler realigned our understanding of our solar system and initiated a surge of discoveries about astronomy.

On this day in 1781, William Herschel discovered Uranus while scanning the heavens for double stars. Our first close up pictures of the planet were taken as Voyager 2 flew by in 1986.

THOUGHT FOR TODAY: Humans have always been curious about the heavens, and now we are gaining a deeper understanding of the universe as we view it through instruments like the Hubble Telescope and visit space with manned and unmanned spaceflight.

MARCH 14: PI DAY

Mathematical science shows what is. It is the language of unseen relations between things.

~ Ada Lovelace ~

Mathematics has been called the language of science. The accurate determination of pi helped people gain a general understanding of the relationship between straight lines and circles. The Babylonians may have been the first to discover this relationship. Archimedes, in the 3rd century BCE, determined pi to a tenth of a percent. Today we calculate pi by using highly technical formulas, but because pi is an irrational number, we can never capture it completely.

THOUGHT FOR TODAY: Mathematics has become so complex that we can accurately calculate the flight of satellites billions of miles away. As the handmaiden of science, math has helped us to understand our world and create beautiful, amazing helpful inventions.

MARCH 15: ENDING CRUEL PUNISHMENTS

In order that punishment should not be an act of violence perpetrated by one or many upon a private citizen, it is essential that it should be public, speedy, necessary.

~ Cesare Beccaria ~

For most of history, punishment was retributive. Sentences meted out were vengeful, meant to directly punish a transgression with violence equal or worse in magnitude.

During the Enlightenment, this brutal regime of punishment was challenged by Cesare Beccaria, who was born this day in 1738. His work *On Crimes and Punishments* argued for a penal system that followed rational principles. He stated that punishment should be used as a preventative deterrent and not a retributive force.

THOUGHT FOR TODAY: For most of human history, prisoners were treated cruelly, underfed and often tortured. While modern prisons are no pleasure palaces, they are more humane and provide opportunities for inmates to reform their lives. Today crime rates are near historic lows, thanks in part to Enlightenment thinking and the work of Cesare Beccaria.

MARCH 16: THE ORIGINAL ROCKET MAN

(Goddard's) rockets...may have been rather crude by present-day standards, but they blazed the trail and incorporated many features used in our most modern rockets.

~ Wernher von Braun ~

The 20th century has many names, including the Space Age. Solid rockets had existed for hundreds of years, thanks to the invention of gunpowder by the Chinese. Liquid-fueled rockets were desirable as tanks and motors could be relatively small. Robert Goddard took an important first step when his liquid rocket lifted off on this day in 1926. During World War II, Wernher von Braun built the infamous V2 rockets for the Nazis. After World War II, he used his expertise for peacetime NASA rocket program, which relied on liquid-fueled rockets.

THOUGHT FOR TODAY: The Space Age was flown (mostly) with rockets propelled by liquid fuels that Goddard pioneered. Goddard could have hardly imagined that 43 years after his rocket's first flight, NASA would put men on the moon.

MARCH 17: THE NATIONAL GALLERY OPENS IN DC

Museums provide places of relaxation and inspiration. And most importantly, they are a place of authenticity.

~ Thomas Campbell ~

On this day in 1941, Franklin Delano Roosevelt opened the National Gallery of Art in Washington, DC. It contained many European and American masterpieces, and, best of all, admission was free. Free museums exist around the world, including the Victoria and Albert Museum, the Museu Afro Brasil, and China's National Museum. Museums are now fundamental national culture, a classroom for children, and a draw for tourism.

 **THOUGHT FOR TODAY:** For most of history, museums did not exist, save as private collections curated for the rich and powerful. Today there are more than 50,000 museums around the world, thousands of which are free or are free on certain days and times. The greatest creations of humankind are available for us to see up close and in person.

MARCH 18: HOMES FOR EVERYONE

Habitat gives us an opportunity which is very difficult to find: to reach out and work side by side with those who never have had a decent home.

~ Jimmy Carter ~

Clarence Jordan came up with his breakthrough idea at Koinonia Farm in Americus, Georgia: partnership housing. Volunteers would work side by side with folks who needed a decent home. His idea worked and thus Habitat for Humanity was born. It formally incorporated under the laws of the state of Georgia on this day in 1977. Habitat for Humanity now serves nearly 1,400 communities in the US and some 70 countries abroad. It has built homes or given shelter to nearly 10 million people since its founding.

THOUGHT FOR TODAY: Thousands of nonprofits are started every year by people who are driven to make the world a better place. Habitat for Humanity, along with many other organizations, has pushed homelessness rates in America lower and lower.

MARCH 19: C-SPAN COVERS THE HOUSE

Democracy must be built through open societies that share information. When there is information, there is enlightenment. When there is debate, there are solutions.

~ Atifete Jahjaga ~

The Cable Satellite Public Affairs Network, better known as C-Span, began broadcasting sessions of the House of Representatives this day in 1979. C-Span is a private not-for-profit organization whose mission, according to their website, is to provide coverage of the House and Senate proceedings, as well as other public affairs content, without "editing, commentary or analysis and with a balanced presentation of points of view."

 **THOUGHT FOR TODAY:** C-Span is one of many initiatives to make government more transparent. Our ability to follow government proceedings means we can keep an eye on our elected officials.

MARCH 20: WORLD WELL-BEING

They are endowed by their Creator with certain unalienable Rights, that among these are Life, Liberty and the pursuit of Happiness

~ The Declaration of Independence ~

The UN General Assembly proclaimed March 20 the International Day of Happiness. In the past, some have ridiculed public policy programs to increase happiness and well-being. William Proxmire, a government waste hawk in the US Senate, once derided a government study about love, deeming it a capricious use of taxpayers' money. More recently, scientific research has demonstrated that there are indeed many things government can do to make its citizens happier, be it promotion of green spaces, parent work leave, or opportunities for better relationships...love.

THOUGHT FOR TODAY: As crime, poverty, disease and illiteracy rates fall, governments are turning to broad policies to make citizens' lives happier.

MARCH 21: A CLEAR CODE FOR A NATION

If we desire respect for the law, we must first make the law respectable.

~ Louis Brandeis ~

On this day in 1804, the Napoleonic Code was adopted in France. It replaced an unruly thatch of laws that had accumulated over centuries. While it was not the first systematic code of laws developed by a nation, it was highly rational and was spread Napoleon's conquests. Many countries adopted the French legal system, and the Napoleonic Code is still law, with revisions, in France.

THOUGHT FOR TODAY: Many people bemoan the legalism of the modern age. Some say Why can't we be ruled by the traditions of old? Because those traditions were inconsistent, unpredictable and often unfair. Modern jurisprudence provides a foundation of precedent, written laws and a well-developed (and public) legal establishment to determine the spirit and letter of the laws.

MARCH 22: CONTRACEPTIVES FOR ALL

Margaret Sanger didn't just introduce the idea of birth control into our culture at large, she freed women from indenture to their bodies.

~ Roxane Gay ~

For most of human history, the life of unmarried women was highly controlled. The emergence of the contraceptive pill in the 1960s gave new freedom for women, but they still had to get a doctor's prescription. Into the 1970s, contraception access was still regulated in much of the US.

On this day in 1972, the Supreme Court ruled in *Eisenstadt v. Baird* that single people could not be denied contraceptives. The court overturned a Massachusetts law that did not allow single people to obtain contraceptives.

THOUGHT FOR TODAY: Besides preventing unwanted children and allowing family planning, easy access to contraception made one of the great delights of life—sex—safer. With Eisenstadt and the global change in mores, the sexual revolution has brought more freedom—and pleasure—to billions.

MARCH 23: OTIS' FIRST ELEVATOR

As we enjoy great advantages from the inventions of others, we should be glad of an opportunity to serve others by any invention of ours.

~ Benjamin Franklin ~

As buildings grew higher and higher during the Industrial Revolution, taking the stairs became less and less appealing. Buildings sometimes installed a windlass outside of a top floor door or window via which heavy deliveries could be hoisted. Powered by steam engines, elevators were installed in buildings in the early 1800s, but many people were wary of using them lest the hoist cable snap.

On this day in 1857, Elisha Otis developed the first safety elevator and installed it in a New York store. Three years earlier he dramatically demonstrated his invention by having the hoist cable severed, and his trademark safety brake arrested the elevator's fall.

THOUGHT FOR TODAY: When humans create a challenge, like taller buildings, we seem to find solutions. Today elevators race up and down buildings more than one hundred stories high.

MARCH 24: SIX PIECES OF PERFECTION

I was obliged to be industrious. Whoever is equally industrious will succeed equally well.

~ Johann Sebastian Bach ~

Some of the most beautiful music of all time was composed in the 18th and 19th century. One of the greatest composers, prolific both the creation of music (1128 pieces) and children (20), was Johann Sebastian Bach. On this day in 1721, Bach dedicated the Brandenburg Concertos, six of his greatest works. In these compositions Bach used a wider array of musical instruments at the height of his considerable powers. Each of the six has sublime properties that had hitherto been untapped in European music.

THOUGHT FOR TODAY: There are thousands of classical music recordings for audiophiles to enjoy. Haydn created 106 symphonies and Mozart composed more than 600 pieces. Today hundreds of symphony orchestras perform classical works for millions of music lovers to enjoy. Enjoy the beauty of musical masterpieces, whether Bach, Be Bop or blues.

MARCH 25: GREEN REVOLUTIONARY

Without food, man can live at most but a few weeks; without it, all other components of social justice are meaningless.

~ Norman Borlaug ~

Norman Borlaug may be the most important person you've never heard of. An agronomist from the Midwest, he worked in Mexico, Pakistan and India to develop plant hybrids and agricultural techniques. His work often doubled and sometimes tripled crop yields. More than anyone else, Borlaug ushered in the Green Revolution that heralded an end to hunger in most of the world. For his efforts he was awarded the Nobel Peace Prize in 1970.

THOUGHT FOR TODAY: Millions, some say at least a billion, lives have been saved because of Borlaug's work on behalf of farmers in developing countries. We live in a time of unprecedented food abundance thanks to Norman Borlaug and other Green Revolutionaries.

MARCH 26: BOB WOODWARD, INVESTIGATIVE JOURNALIST

I believe Watergate shows that the system did work. Particularly the Judiciary and the Congress, and ultimately an independent prosecutor.

~ Bob Woodward ~

The pen is mightier than the sword may seem an empty bromide, but in the early 1970s, two journalists at *The Washington Post* made a strong argument for the power of journalism. Bob Woodward, born on this day in 1943, and Carl Bernstein uncovered crimes that the Nixon Administration perpetrated in its bid for reelection. In their original investigative journalism, they uncovered felonies committed under the leadership of President Nixon. While the revelations shocked American and shook its democracy, journalism proved itself to be an effective check on presidential overreach.

THOUGHT FOR TODAY: For most of history kings and emperors ruled by fiat and could execute opponents at will. In the 21st century, elected leaders are circumscribed by laws that they must follow, and an active, independent press is a check on their power.

MARCH 27: TYPHOID MARY QUARANTINED!

We must treat those suffering from disease in an intelligent, humane, and compassionate way. We need to be rational and keep our fears in check.

~ Susan Campbell Bartoletti ~

Typhoid is spread by ingesting food or drink contaminated by fecal matter. People often associate the disease with Typhoid Mary—Mary Mallon—a cook who spread the disease in the early 20th century. Since this was before typhoid vaccines and antibiotics, Typhoid Mary was quarantined for nearly thirty years of her life; her last quarantine began on this date in 1915.

THOUGHT FOR TODAY: At the turn of the 20th century, more than 33 of every 100,000 Americans died each year from typhoid fever, according to CDC records. Today in the United States there are few cases and no deaths. It is easy to forget that communicable diseases cut down Americans like a scythe until public health laws, vaccines and antibiotics became widespread in the latter half of the 20th century.

MARCH 28: DEVELOPING COUNTRIES OVERTAKE THE RICH ONES

We've taken the view that if the rest of the world would democratize and create market economies, that would spread the benefits of prosperity around the world.

~ Jeffrey Sachs ~

On or around this day in 2012, developing countries surpassed rich ones in total GDP. Much of this can be explained by the explosive growth of the two most populous countries in the world, India and China. But countries in other parts of the world, including Latin America and Africa, have also been developing at a rapid rate. In fact, in some parts of Africa, cell phone penetration is higher than it is in rich countries.

THOUGHT FOR TODAY: Many people still believe that the developing world is a place of abject poverty and little hope. In reality, places like sub-Saharan Africa and Asia have been growing faster than developed countries.

MARCH 29: THE HARVARD MARK I

Don't worry about people stealing your ideas. If your ideas are any good, you'll have to ram them down people's throats.

~ Howard Aiken ~

Our current era is known as the Information Age because of the power of our machines to collect, store, process and send information. An important milestone was the creation of the Harvard Mark I computer. On this day in 1944, the Mark I completed an important calculation for the Manhattan Project.

The Mark I team, led by Howard Aiken, created the first fully functioning computer. This IBM machine advanced the field of computing and was followed by the Mark II, III and IV.

THOUGHT FOR TODAY: Today's iPhones have more computation power and complexity than the Mark I computer. IBM's early breakthroughs were only used by scientists, mathematicians and engineers, but now billions of people carry high power computers in their pockets and purses.

MARCH 30: BLACK BEAUTY ENERGIZES A MOVEMENT

My doctrine is this, that if we see cruelty or wrong that we have the power to stop, and do nothing, we make ourselves sharers in the guilt.

~ Anna Sewell ~

The history of animal cruelty is a long one. Today animals are treated much more humanely than in the past, thanks to the rise of popular reform movements. One milestone was the publication of *Black Beauty* in 1877. Anna Sewell, who was born on this day in 1820, wrote it not for children but for adults who handled animals. It became a children's classic, one of the bestselling novels in the English language. In direct response to the popularity of *Black Beauty*, organizations and laws sprang up for the protection of animals.

THOUGHT FOR TODAY: Animal cruelty, once shrugged off as a timeless aspect of civilization, is now seen as barbaric. In rich countries, animal adoption is a new norm to both save beleaguered pets from abandonment and to avoid participation in the puppy mill industry.

MARCH 31: CÉSAR CHÁVEZ, LABOR LEADER

If you really want to make a friend, go to someone's house and eat with him. The people who give you their food give you their heart.

~ César Chávez ~

As a labor leader and leading light in the Latino rights movement, César Chávez was peerless. As a young man he dropped out of school and became a migrant farm worker until 1952, when he started organizing. With Dolores Huerta, he founded the United Farm Workers Union. He also organized boycotts and strikes that led to recognition of farm worker rights. While the success of specific actions remains in dispute, he undoubtedly raised awareness of the rights of farm workers and the Latino community.

THOUGHT FOR TODAY: Many social movements have highlighted the particular challenges and struggles of the many Americas. Today we do what we can to lift all communities—all Americans—so that everyone has a place at the table.

APRIL 1: FIRST SALARIED FIRE DEPARTMENT ESTABLISHED

When firefighters go to the office, we might birth a baby in the morning, save a drowning surfer in the afternoon, and run into a fire at night.

~ Caroline Paul ~

House fires have killed millions over the millennia. Because fire was used for home heating and cooking, stray sparks often led to deadly conflagrations. To respond to this danger, fire companies formed in cities, though most were manned by volunteers. On this day in 1853, the first salaried fire department was established in Cincinnati, Ohio. Thousands of professional fire departments were established during the 19th and 20th centuries. Today, most communities around the world are served by professional firefighters.

THOUGHT FOR TODAY: The threat of house fire has been a deadly feature of life for thousands of years. But in recent times house fires have become much less frequent and deadly thanks to smoke alarms, flame retardant materials, and the proliferation of professional fire departments.

APRIL 2: AN INFORMATION REVOLUTION

Whenever culture has gone through a radical change, as ours has - from industrial age to information age - there are people who will deny that things have changed.

~ Daniel Greenberg ~

Legal libraries are synonymous with dusty shelves and rows of leather bound books. Searching through hundreds of books for legal precedents was difficult, time consuming and expensive. But the Information Age changed the nature of legal research. On this day in 1973, the pioneer legal database LexisNexis went online for a pilot program in Ohio and Texas. Within ten years all US laws and codes were available online.

The database revolution changed nearly every industry and academic field. Nowadays, anyone who has access to the internet can find information on almost any topic.

 **THOUGHT FOR TODAY:** Just as humans were freed by the advance of democracy and human rights, so too has information been freed by computers and the internet. This freedom benefits us by making information accessible and inexpensive.

APRIL 3: TRAIN SPEED RECORD

I like trains. I like their rhythm, and I like the freedom of being suspended between two places, all anxieties of purpose taken care of.

~ Anna Funder ~

In many parts of the world, cars and buses now play the mass transit role that trains once played. But innovations in train technology in the past half-century have brought trains roaring back. In 1964, Japanese bullet trains that traveled at speeds around 150 miles per hour began service. France started it TGV service in 1981. Today China runs the largest system of high-speed trains.

On this date in 2007, the French LGV train reached a maximum speed of 357 miles per hour during a test. Chinese high-speed trains later broke this record. Innovations continue apace and speed records continue to fall.

THOUGHT FOR TODAY: High speed trains are much safer than driving and prevent thousands of highway deaths around the world. They use less energy per passenger mile and get riders to their destinations faster than cars and buses do.

APRIL 4: ADVOCATE FOR THE MENTALLY ILL

In a world where there is so much to be done. I felt strongly impressed that there must be something for me to do.

~ Dorothea Dix ~

On this day in 1802, reformer Dorothea Dix was born in Hampden, Maine. After witnessing the poor treatment of the mentally ill in Europe, she returned to America and began a life of activism. Dix inspected Massachusetts hospitals for the mentally ill and reported her findings to the legislature; her efforts led to institutional reforms. During the Civil War she became the head of Army nurses and brought her trailblazing reform spirit to the improvement of the nursing profession.

THOUGHT FOR TODAY: Despite poor health and bouts of depression, Dix worked tirelessly on the behalf of the mentally ill. Thanks to pioneers like Dorothea Dix, the care of people with mental illness is light years ahead of where it was just a few generations ago.

APRIL 5: THE CCC IS SIGNED INTO EXISTENCE

Growing up during the Depression, I worked for the Forest Service and CCC. I tend to work very, very hard. I wouldn't change that for anything.

~ Raymond Burr ~

The Great Depression of the 1930s was a gut punch to workers in the US and around the world. Unemployment rates in the United States got as high as 25%. One of Roosevelt's most successful job programs was the Civilian Conservation Corps (CCC), established on this day in 1933. Young men worked in CCC camps to plant trees, construct buildings in National Parks, and build roads like the Blue Ridge Parkway. Many of the iconic structures in National Parks were built by the boys of the CCC.

THOUGHT FOR TODAY: Work programs like the CCC helped counter the hopelessness of young men during the Great Depression. Many would send their relatively meager wages home to help their struggling families. Talk to a CCC veteran and you will hear stories of growth and gratitude for government help through hard times.

APRIL 6: RACE TO THE NORTH POLE

I think I'm the first man to sit on top of the world.

~ Matthew Henson ~

On this day in 1909, Robert Peary and Matthew Henson became the first people to reach the North Pole. Their partnership formed more than 20 years before. Peary, a white naval officer, was recruiting men to build a canal in Nicaragua. He met Henson, an experienced black seaman, and was quickly impressed with his knowledge and experience.

But because he was black, Henson received little recognition while Peary earned international accolades. In 1988, Henson was finally given his rightful place in history. His remains were moved to Arlington National Cemetery, and he was buried with full honors.

THOUGHT FOR TODAY: In some respects, history has been whitewashed to emphasis the accomplishments of whites. In fits and starts, a broader, more inclusive (and accurate) tapestry of history is being woven that reflects everyone's heritage and achievements.

APRIL 7: GAY RIGHTS ACTIVIST HARRY HAY

I knew that I was gay in every bone of my body. So I did the only thing I could do. I started the movement.

~ Harry Hay ~

Before the Stonewall Riots in 1969, the gays rights movement was closeted by heterosexist laws and culture. Twenty years before, Harry Hay and friends founded the Mattachine Society. Hay knew he was gay from an early age, but he tried to assimilate by marrying a woman and starting a family. He was inspired by the Kinsey Report, which demonstrated that homosexuality was much more widespread that had been previously believed. In the Mattachine Society and many other efforts, Hay tirelessly fought for gay rights and culture until his death in 2000.

THOUGHT FOR TODAY: Gay rights have come a long way thanks to the work of activists like Harry Hay, who was born on this day in 1912. Today gays can marry, and discrimination, though it still exists, has been successfully undone in many places.

APRIL 8: FIRST DAY OF NATIONAL CRIME VICTIMS' RIGHTS WEEK

Our police officers put their lives on the line every single day. They've got a tough job to do to maintain public safety and hold accountable those who break the law.

~ Barack Obama ~

When polled about their perceptions of crime, most Americans think it's getting worse. Nothing can be further from the truth. Crime rates fell precipitously between 1995 and 2015. For every 15 aggravated assaults in 1995, there were only three in 2015. Rape and sexual assault were cut in half, and robbery rates were only a third of what they had been 20 years previously.

THOUGHT FOR TODAY: TV news, especially local stations, reports a daily drum roll of crime, which leads many to believe that crime is getting worse. On the contrary, crime rates are near historic lows in most places in the US and the world. The next time you see a police office, thank them for keeping us safe.

APRIL 9: MARIAN SINGS WITH MR. LINCOLN

There are many persons ready to do what is right because in their hearts they know it is right. But they hesitate, waiting for the other fellow to make the first move.

~ Marian Anderson ~

The grip of racism in America relaxed slowly and only with great effort. On this day in 1865, Confederate Robert E. Lee surrendered to Ulysses S. Grant. Union victory ended slavery but not the struggle for freedom. In 1939, soprano Marian Anderson was set to sing at the Daughters of the American Revolution (DAR) Constitution Hall in Washington, DC, but she was not allowed to because she was black. First Lady Eleanor Roosevelt, herself a DAR, resigned her membership and invited Anderson to sing in front of the Lincoln Memorial on this day in 1939.

THOUGHT FOR TODAY: The road to equality has been long, but with the passing of time rights continue to expand. In the 21st century African Americans have risen to the highest offices in all branches of government.

APRIL 10: GOOD FRIDAY AGREEMENT SIGNED

I believe there's no such thing as a conflict that can't be ended. They're created and sustained by human beings. They can be ended by human beings.

~ George Mitchell ~

On this day in 1998, the Good Friday Agreement was signed in Belfast, Northern Ireland. It ended 30 years of sectarian conflict and violence, known as "The Troubles." While imperfect, the agreement charted a devolved government structure that has stood for nearly two decades. Most important, there has been much less violence and terrorism since the agreement was signed.

 **THOUGHT FOR TODAY:** In the late 20th century, "The Troubles" of Northern Ireland were synonymous with intractable conflict. Nonetheless, the conflict has proved to be tractable, which demonstrates that conflicts can be resolved in a peaceful manner despite the skepticism of warring parties and citizens.

APRIL 11: MAN'S BEST FRIEND

Isn't it strange that, our being such an intelligent primate, we didn't domesticate chimpanzees as companions instead?

~ Wolfgang Schleidt ~

At least 15,000 years ago, humans domesticated dogs. There are many contested theories about how dogs were domesticated, but it can be surmised that as humans and dogs started to live together, people began to selectively breed them for traits the humans wanted, be it hunting prowess, protection or companionship. The two species have co-evolved such that dogs can easily read human emotions and vice versa.

THOUGHT FOR TODAY: Today is National Pet Day. Most people who keep dogs and other pets do so for companionship. This ever-strengthening bond between humans and pets can be seen in the increased expenditure people are lavishing on their pets, be it toys, food or veterinary care. People who keep pets tend to be happier, healthier and live longer.

APRIL 12: A BIG DAY IN SPACE

When I orbited the Earth in a spaceship, I saw for the first time how beautiful our planet is. Mankind, let us preserve and increase this beauty, and not destroy it!

~ Yuri Gagarin ~

Space travel was a pie in the sky dream until Yuri Gagarin flew into the great beyond on this day in 1961. This achievement was all the greater because Gagarin and his craft, *Vostok 1,* orbited the earth and returned safely, something NASA would not complete until John Glenn's flight in *Friendship 7* one year later.

As of late 2017, there have been more than 300 manned space flights that reached orbit. Today there is a constant presence in space at the International Space Station, and plans are underway for a mission to Mars.

THOUGHT FOR TODAY: Yuri Gagarin's successful space flight in 1961 started human travel in the Space Age. Human curiosity and scientific progress continue to push boundaries here on earth and beyond.

APRIL 13: GPS IS BORN

In places like India with smartphones, there's an app now for women if they're in a violent situation, they can press a button to say "Here I am."

~ Melinda Gates ~

Soon after Sputnik was launched into space, the United States learned to track the satellite by factoring in shifts in its radio signal caused by the doppler effect. The US Navy applied these insights to developing a system of satellites tracking its nuclear submarines around the globe. Experiments in the 1960s led to the development of a tracking system consisting of six satellites.

In the 70s and 80s, the Department of Defense would use the insights gleaned from the Navy's tracking system to develop a more comprehensive global positioning system that was fully implemented by the early 90s.

THOUGHT FOR TODAY: Anyone with a smartphone has access to GPS. Besides guiding people to their destinations, it helps find lost people, manage car and truck fleets, make law enforcement more effective, and protect soldiers during deployment.

APRIL 14: THE HUMAN GENOME IS SEQUENCED

The ever-quickening advances of science made possible by the success of the Human Genome Project will also soon let us see the essences of mental disease.

~ James D. Watson ~

On this day in 2003, the National Human Genome Research Institute announced the completion of the human genome sequence. This was almost exactly 50 years after Watson and Crick described the double helix structure of DNA. This project was considered a scientific moonshot, an audacious goal to map human genetics. What seemed like impossible science fiction even in the early 1990s became reality a decade later.

 **THOUGHT FOR TODAY:** From Gregor Mendel, to Watson and Crick, to the sequencing of the human genome, our understanding of genetics is slaking our thirst for knowledge of our past and improving our health now and into the future.

APRIL 15: SCHOOL FOR THE DEAF FOUNDED IN HARTFORD

The problem is not that the students do not hear. The problem is that the hearing world does not listen.

~ Jesse Jackson ~

Thomas Gallaudet, Mason Cogswell and Laurent Clerc founded The American School for the Deaf (ASD) on this day in 1817. ASD is the oldest permanent school for the deaf in the United States. Laurent Clerc brought French Sign Language to America, which developed into American Sign Language. Today hundreds of schools for the deaf exist, and millions of deaf and hearing people use sign language.

THOUGHT FOR TODAY: Aristotle reflected the prejudices of many when he said, "Deaf people could not be educated (because) without hearing, people could not learn." Hearing impaired geniuses like Beethoven and Thomas Edison proved that intellect and hearing ability were not related. Today deaf people and deaf culture have been embraced after millennia of persecution.

APRIL 16: COLD AFTER HOT

I grew up during the Cold War, when everything seemed very tenuous. For many years I had vivid nightmares of nuclear apocalypse.

~ Justin Cronin ~

The world celebrated the end of World War II after Germany and Japan were utterly defeated. Unfortunately, the late 40s saw the rise of a new war between the capitalist and democratic West and the communist and authoritarian East.

On this day in 1947, Bernard Baruch gave a speech in which he said, "Let us not be deceived: we are today in the midst of a cold war." The term stuck. For the next forty-plus years, the Cold War between the West and East ebbed and flowed until it ended quite suddenly around 1990.

THOUGHT FOR TODAY: Some claim that terrorist threats make the world more dangerous than ever. How quickly they forget the days of Mutual Assured Destruction (MAD)! Contrary to doomsday descriptions, evidence demonstrates that the current age is the most peaceful one of all time.

APRIL 17: BEER IS BACK IN AMERICA!

I have a total irreverence for anything connected with society except that which makes the roads safer, the beer stronger, the food cheaper.

~ Brendan Behan ~

The 18th Amendment of the Constitution outlawed alcoholic beverages in the US. It led to an alcohol black market that fueled gangsterism and (often fatal) bathtub gin. But the 21st Amendment ended Prohibition and brought all liquor, wine and beer back to America.

Not that American beer was any good. Most beers from the US were weak lagers until the craft and microbrewery industry started growing in the 80s. America, once known as a beer desert, now is the home of some of the best beer in the world.

THOUGHT FOR TODAY: Many gourmet industries—wine, beer, cheese, cigars and heirloom vegetables—have increased in popularity despite the dominance of giant food multinationals. According to Joe Satran in The Huffington Post, there were only 42 breweries in the US in 1979. Today there are more than 2000.

APRIL 18: A HIGH COURT COMES TO ORDER

When there is no sharing of power, no rule of law, no accountability, there is abuse, corruption, subjugation and indignation.

~ Atifete Jahjaga ~

The right to a fair trial is a relatively recent development. Judges often dispensed "justice" that fulfilled a monarch's wishes. In recent centuries independent judiciaries have become more common, keeping kings, presidents and premiers in line.

In the 20th century, international courts came into existence. On this day in 1946, the International Court of Justice (ICJ) met for the first time. The court has very limited jurisdiction, but neither did the first parliaments. If nothing else, the existence of the ICJ reflects the widespread view that all nations should follow standards of law.

THOUGHT FOR TODAY: The rule of law is a hallmark of modernity. Leaders often push the limits of the rule of law, but democratic norms and institutions continue to spread and grow around the world.

APRIL 19: SEX AND JAIL

Good sex is like good bridge. If you don't have a good partner, you'd better have a good hand.

~ Mae West ~

Brilliant, beautiful, and sexy, Mae West blazed a trail on stage and screen that no other women had trod in America. With breezy confidence, West's double entendres and innuendos were shocking as much as they were hilarious. Such sexual liberty from a woman, especially done with aplomb and no shame, was unheard of in mass entertainment.

On this day in 1927, Mae West was sentenced to ten days in jail for her Broadway play *Sex*. While the bawdy play received scathing reviews from the press, it was the most popular show on Broadway during its run.

THOUGHT FOR TODAY: Until very recently, sexual mores nearly everywhere meant that women had little freedom to express their sexuality in their own ways. Today women have more sexual freedom than ever.

APRIL 20: RELIGIOUS FREEDOM GRANTED

We must overcome anti-Semitism and the prejudice that divides us. We must defeat Islamophobia and the fears that weaken us.

~ Ban Ki-moon ~

Many minorities have been mistreated in the past, but Jews have been particularly ill-treated. After being oppressed by Egyptians, Babylonians, and Greeks the Romans expelled them from Israel.

Dispersed around the Mediterranean, Jews were still persecuted in their new homes. In the mid-1600s, two dozen Jews settled in New Amsterdam—now New York City—as refugees. At first the Dutch authorities opposed religious freedom, but on this day in 1657, religious freedom was granted to the Jews of New Amsterdam. Today more than a million and a half Jews live in and around New York City.

THOUGHT FOR TODAY: Prejudice has not been fully conquered, but the history of Jewish survival is an inspiring tale of resilience. All too slowly, most of the world is seeing the wrongs of antisemitism.

APRIL 21: PLANETS BEYOND OUR SOLAR SYSTEM

How vast those Orbs must be, and how inconsiderable this Earth, the Theatre upon which all our mighty Designs are transacted.

~ Christiaan Huygens ~

Outer space is typified by one quality: space. Lots of space. A bright, burning sun may be orbited by planets, but those tend to be billions of miles away.

Given these great distances, and the relative tininess of planets, it is hard to imagine astronomers finding planets beyond our solar system. But on this day in 1992, that's exactly what happened. Aleksander Wolszczan and Dale Frail discovered planets orbiting a pulsar 2300 light years away.

THOUGHT FOR TODAY: As we learn more about the cosmos we learn more about ourselves. If planets exist around the billions of stars in the universe, then surely other places host life. It draws us ever outward to space, the place where innumerable wonders await discovery.

APRIL 22: EARTH DAY

Cherish these natural wonders, cherish the natural resources, cherish the history and romance as a sacred heritage, for your children and your children's children.

~ *Theodore Roosevelt* ~

In early 1969, millions of gallons of oil spilled off the coast of Southern California. Later that year the Cuyahoga River caught fire as chemicals and oil ignited on the water's surface. DDT was decimating bird populations, including the bald eagle, America's national symbol.

These events galvanized environmentalists, led by Senator Gaylord Nelson and his associate Denis Hayes, to organize the first Earth Day on April 22, 1970. Gatherings in New York, Washington and other cities birthed the modern environmental movement, which grew into the powerful public force for planetary protection.

THOUGHT FOR TODAY: By most measures—global warming excepted—air and water quality have improved. Citizens around the world are composting waste, farming organically, and supporting greener laws and lifestyles.

APRIL 23: SCHOOLS FOR ALL CHILDREN

Upon the subject of education, I can only say that I view it as the most important subject which we as a people may be engaged in.

~ Abraham Lincoln ~

For most of history, education was only accessible to the wealthy. In Europe, the Protestant Reformation expanded literacy as people were expected to read scriptures. Literacy was high in the New England colonies because reading was seen as desirable to expand the study of the Bible. The first free school in the colonies was Boston Latin School, which opened this day in 1635.

Public education spread throughout the world in the 19th and 20th century. Literacy and numeracy have expanded to most people on the planet.

THOUGHT FOR TODAY: Education was once a rare luxury. Today most children in the world, regardless of their wealth or citizenship, complete some school. In the United States more than 80% of high school students earn a diploma, and graduation rates continue to climb.

APRIL 24: THE GREATEST TELESCOPE OF ALL TIME

A Hubble Space Telescope photograph of the universe evokes far more awe for creation than light streaming through a stained-glass window in a cathedral.

~ Michael Shermer ~

The greatest telescope of all is still going strong, far outliving its projected lifespan. On this day in 1990, the Hubble Space Telescope deployed from Space Shuttle *Discovery*. It had an inauspicious start. A flaw in the mirror meant that it did not work fully until 1993, but it has been wowing humanity ever since. The Hubble telescope helped scientists discover that the universe's expansion is accelerating rather than slowing and that supermassive black holes exist in the center of most galaxies.

THOUGHT FOR TODAY: Incredible technological achievements like the Hubble Space Telescope have led to earth-shattering discoveries about the universe. Hubble's successor, The James Webb Space Telescope, will be launched in 2019. It will undoubtedly surpass the incredible discoveries made by Hubble.

APRIL 25: A MEETING ON THE ELBE

This world of ours must avoid becoming a community of dreadful fear and hate, and be, instead, a proud confederation of mutual trust and respect.

~ Dwight D. Eisenhower ~

On this day in 1945, Russian and Allied forces met at the Elbe River. This juncture marked the end of the worst period of human history, which preceded the best and worst of times. It was the best of times for the countries freed from fascism. But grim times lay ahead in The Soviet Union and in China, where Mao would persecute opponents and starve millions of his own citizens. In the late 1980s Communist countries fell like dominoes, and since then the world has gotten richer, healthier, more literate, longer lived and freer.

THOUGHT FOR TODAY: Many people fret about the state of the world, but in our current age there is much less conflict than there was during the Cold War. No major powers are at war, and wars are becoming less frequent and less deadly.

APRIL 26: GLOBAL TRADE ON STEROIDS

Globalization and free trade do spur economic growth, and they lead to lower prices on many goods.

~ Robert Reich ~

The invention of the caravel and open ocean sailing ships brought the world together in news ways. More recently, the invention of the shipping container increased the efficiency and volume of global trade. On this day in 1956 the first successful container ship left the port of Newark for Houston.

Shipping containers were revolutionary because they improved efficiency. Containers were loaded on and off of ships and then put directly onto the backs of freight cars or trucks. By making trade faster and cheaper, both producers and consumers benefited.

THOUGHT FOR TODAY: Global trade has made life better in many ways. Besides making more food and goods available to everyone, the decreasing prices of these goods has made survival easier.

APRIL 27: THE SPREAD OF UNIVERSITIES IN AMERICA

The land-grant university system is being built on behalf of the people.

~ Abraham Lincoln ~

Today there are more than 25,000 universities in the world. The first were founded in the Middle Ages, including the Sorbonne, Oxford, and the University of Heidelberg. Nonetheless, these institutions remained out of reach for all but a few. In 1862, the Morrill Act expanded access to higher education in the US via land grant universities.

Cornell University, which was created as a land grant university on this day in 1865, was one of the early pioneers. Like other land grant universities, it focused on agricultural and mechanical sciences, unlike traditional religious or liberal arts universities.

THOUGHT FOR TODAY: Today more than half of Americans get some university education. The land grant universities created during the 1800s expanded college education to the masses. University education continues to expand and improve the lives of people around the world.

APRIL 28: OCCUPATIONAL SAFETY AND HEALTH ADMINISTRATION FOUNDED

Working safely may get old, but so do those who practice it.

~ Anonymous ~

In the early 1970s, 14,000 US workers were killed on the job each year. Today that number has dropped to about 5,000 despite today's larger workforce. Jobs have gotten safer as safety standards have improved. Nowadays it is much more common for workers to don their orange safety gear and hardhats. While workplaces can never be made perfectly safe, the dramatic decrease in workplace fatalities and injuries are due in part to worker safety initiatives like the Occupational Safety and Health Administration (OSHA).

THOUGHT FOR TODAY: When you go to work or see construction workers doing their job, consider the fact that on-the-job deaths have decreased more than two-thirds in the last two generations. This is one of those "invisible" statistics that many people are not aware of, yet it demonstrates how life keeps getting better—and safer.

APRIL 29: LONG BEAUTIFUL HAIR

I've discovered that Motown and Broadway have a lot in common - a family of wonderfully talented, passionate, hardworking young people.

~ Berry Gordy ~

Broadway musicals both reflect and act as a bellwether of American culture. Such was the success with Hair, which debuted at the Biltmore Theater on this day in 1968. It was a celebration of hippie love, sex, drugs and Black Power. In earlier eras Hair might have faced persecution, as happened with Mae West's Sex (see April 19). But in a more open and liberal time, Hair became mainstream.

THOUGHT FOR TODAY: Just as Mae West's Sex shocked in the 1920s, and West Side Story broke new ground in the 1950s, Hair raised hackles but was just one of many Broadway productions that expanded horizons. Today Hair seems somewhat tame, but it pushed the boundaries of sexual freedom and protested the Vietnam War. In a democracy, theater can teach, entertain and change perspectives.

APRIL 30: THE FUHRER'S DEATH

In many ways, Nazism was antithetical to what the great mass of Germans admired.

~ Eugene Davidson ~

Who was the worst devil in human history? Adolf Hitler tops most lists because of the scope of his genocidal barbarism. On this day Hitler killed himself in his bunker beneath Berlin. We hope there will never be another conflict like World War II, but to prevent the rise of another populist like Hitler, we must support democracy, human rights, rule of law, and thwart nationalism and bigotry.

THOUGHT FOR TODAY: World War II was a nightmare, but like all nightmares, it ended. Since this terrible conflict, the world has seen the longest sustained period of global peace in history. Tensions rise and fall, but no great powers are on the verge of invading their neighbors. Though egregious crimes against humanity still occur, they have been decreasing.

MAY 1: THE AMAZING ICELANDIC GENOME

The goal of getting your genome done is not to tell you what you will die from, but it's how to learn how to take action to prevent disease.

~ George M. Church ~

Iceland is a small, isolated country whose inhabitants can trace their ancestry back to a few common founders...all of which makes the country an excellent genetics laboratory. Add a national system of carefully collected medical records and meticulous genealogical records, *et voilà*, it's time to start experimenting.

The May 2015 edition of *Nature Genetics* featured four articles about the Icelandic genome. One study discovered a gene associated with Alzheimer's disease, while another found the most recent male relative shared by all humans. Studies from this tiny island country will have implications for gene testing, therapies and the science of genetics.

THOUGHT FOR TODAY: Scientists find ingenious ways to expand the frontiers of human understanding. Geneticists are capitalizing on opportunity the Icelandic genome provides, and the findings will likely offer insights that will benefit all of humanity.

MAY 2: DR. SPOCK

What good mothers and fathers instinctively feel like doing for their babies is the best after all.

~ Benjamin Spock ~

In the mid-20th century, the dominant child-rearing philosophy in America was promoted by John B. Watson. He thought that a mother's love was "a dangerous instrument...which may make infancy unhappy, adolescence a nightmare."

Luckily for us, and millions of children, Benjamin Spock wrote a book that extolled the opposite philosophy. Dr. Spock, who was born this day in 1903, reassured mothers that "you know more than you think you do." Spock encouraged common sense parenting and treating children as individuals.

THOUGHT FOR TODAY: Spock brought warmth back to parenting at a time when "experts" like Watson and Freud believed that mothers could have a negative effect on children. Today, from more than 50 years of research, we know that warm, loving parenting is necessary for children to thrive.

MAY 3: HOW THE OTHER HALF LIVES

No society can surely be flourishing and happy, of which the far greater part of the members are poor and miserable.

~ Adam Smith ~

For most of history, the poor were often vilified as lazy or mollified with handouts. Reform movements in the 1800s, often in response to urban squalor, tried to raise living standards. Concern for the urban poor was ignited by the work of Jacob Riis, who was born on this day in 1849.

Riis used the new technology of flash photography to capture the lives of children toiling in sweatshops. Riis' journalism had a powerful positive impact, including the New York Tenement House Acts, which required that new tenements have more light, ventilation and space.

THOUGHT FOR TODAY: Photojournalism, of which Jacob Riis was a pioneer, has become a powerful force in exposing social ills and creating positive change. Photojournalists bring the public closer to places that are hard to look at but need to be seen.

MAY 4: FOUNDER OF THE SETTLEMENT MOVEMENT

America's future will be determined by the home and the school. The child becomes largely what he is taught; hence we must watch what we teach, and how we live.

~ Jane Addams ~

Henrietta Barnett, who was born on this day in 1851, made helping the poor her life's work. In 1884, she and her husband started the first settlement house, a place for rich and poor to live together, gain a good education, and pursue self-improvement. The movement spread through England and into America, where Hull House in Chicago was the best-known settlement house. University Settlement in New York had many famous alumni, including Andrew Carnegie, George and Ira Gershwin, and Gifford Pinchot.

THOUGHT FOR TODAY: Social movements and government programs have done much to improve the lot of the poor, which is reflected in poverty statistics. For all of history until the 1800s, more than 90% of the world population lived in abject poverty. Today that figure is less than 10%.

MAY 5: THE INVENTIVE MARY KIES

Courage doesn't always roar. Sometimes courage is the quiet voice at the end of the day saying, "I will try again tomorrow."

~ Mary Anne Radmacher ~

Women have been inventing things since the beginning of time, but they rarely received the credit for their work. In the 1700s, many women were forbidden from filing and holding patents. On this day in 1809, Mary Kies was the first woman to be granted a patent in the US. She developed a new method of spinning straw to make bonnets, a particularly important invention as there was a limited supply of thread and cloth due to the Napoleonic Wars.

THOUGHT FOR TODAY: Nowadays, the percentage of patents held by women is much higher than it was 200 years ago, but, at about 20%, it is still very low given the progress that has been made toward gender equality in other areas. While barriers to sex equality still exist, progress continues today.

MAY 6: THE CHUNNEL OPENS

At its heart, engineering is about using science to find creative, practical solutions. It is a noble profession.

~ Queen Elizabeth II ~

England's isolation from Europe has meant it has eluded conquest for nearly 1000 years. On this day in 1994, a new link between the island nation and the continent was made official. Queen Elizabeth II traveled east through the new Channel Tunnel, popularly known as the Chunnel, while French President François Mitterrand traveled west. The trains met nose to nose, signaling the completed link between France and England.

Today more than 20 million people travel through the Chunnel each year. The American Society of Civil Engineers has called the Chunnel one of the seven modern Wonders of the World.

THOUGHT FOR TODAY: Through daring visions, innovation and hard work, humans continue to bridge chasms that once isolated us. It is hard to imagine the limits of human ingenuity.

MAY 7: THE INTEGRATED CIRCUIT IS CONCEIVED

With the advent of the transistor, it seems now possible to envisage electronic equipment in a solid block with no connecting wires.

~ Geoffrey Dummer ~

An important theme in electronics is the drive to make the building blocks of an electrical system denser and more compact. In doing this, electrical contraptions become more powerful. The creation of the vacuum tube in 1904 was once such leap, as was the transistor. The building block of the current computer age is the microprocessor.

On this day in 1952, Geoffrey Dummer gave a presentation about the possibility of the integrated circuit at a conference in Washington, DC. This beautiful idea was made real, and patented, by Jack Kilby six years later. Kilby received credit for the integrated circuit, but Dummer's insight made it possible.

THOUGHT FOR TODAY: Every smart technology that makes our lives safer and better—computers, smartphones, HVAC systems—runs on integrated circuits. Often unseen, these microchips give us many benefits.

MAY 8: SMALLPOX ERADICATED

In 1967, the world health community launched a global effort to eradicate smallpox. It took a coordinated, worldwide effort. By 1977, smallpox had disappeared.

~ Liya Kebede ~

On this date in 1980, the World Health Assembly declared smallpox to be eradicated. This scourge had killed millions over the millennia, including Pocahontas and King Louis XV of France. Inoculation practices started a thousand years ago in China and spread to most parts of the world. By 1796, English doctor Edward Jenner developed an effective inoculation. Modern vaccines were developed by 1900 and momentum toward eradication picked up speed. After World War II, the World Health Organization coordinated eradication efforts, and by the late 70s, the last cases were reported.

THOUGHT FOR TODAY: Killer diseases that bring dread to humanity are being eradicated by the unstinting efforts of doctors, public health organizations, and NGOs. Longevity and human health continue to improve as medical progress pushes back the scourge of disease.

MAY 9: A VAST WASTELAND

Public broadcasting is for all Americans. It can meet the needs of audiences that number in the millions but are seldom served anywhere else.

~ Jimmy Carter ~

In the 1950s, nearly all television content was produced by NBC, CBS and ABC. Television had a few gems like *I Love Lucy* and *The Honeymooners*, but much of the programming was inferior. On this day in 1961, FCC chairman Newton Minow criticized TV by saying "when television is bad, nothing is worse. I invite each of you to sit down in front of your own television set when your station goes on the air and stay there, for a day. I can assure you that what you will observe is a vast wasteland."

 **THOUGHT FOR TODAY:** Minow's "Vast Wasteland" speech was a turning point that led to the creation of the Public Broadcasting Corporation (PBS). In the 21st Century, new television from HBO, Netflix and Amazon lead many to claim that TV has never been better.

MAY 10: FINANCIAL PANIC!

Unemployment insurance, the 40-hour work week, collective bargaining, strong banking regulations, and job programs were all described as 'socialist.'

~ Bernie Sanders ~

O n this day on 1837, banks in New York City refused to give payment to its customers because of a financial panic. The government chose not to intervene, and the brunt of the panic was felt by workers and business owners. Panics like these continued through for the next hundred years, including the Panic of 1857, the Panic of 1873, and the Great Depression.

In the 20th Century, financial regulation and the Federal Reserve System stabilized the financial system. Roosevelt's New Deal added job programs that further ballasted the economy.

THOUGHT FOR TODAY: During the first 150 years of US history, recessions and bank panics were more severe and more frequent. Since then, central banks have stabilized and regulated markets. While bubbles and panics still occur, none have been as destructive as the ones before World War II.

MAY 11: CHARGES DISMISSED

We were young, we were foolish, we were arrogant, but we were right.

~ Daniel Ellsberg ~

Daniel Ellsberg was one of the most famous leakers of all time. Leaking—releasing secret documents to influence policy or politics—was and is very controversial. Ellsberg leaked the so-called Pentagon Papers, which revealed that the US government had been deceptive about its conduct of the Vietnam War. Charges were brought against him for leaking documents, but Judge William M. Byrne dropped them because he deemed that government misconduct justified what Ellsberg had done.

THOUGHT FOR TODAY: For most of history, kings, pharaohs and emperors could break the law with impunity. Today leaders are expected to follow the law and are often punished or embarrassed when they don't. Leaking of documents remains controversial to this day, but the threat of leaks often deters misconduct.

MAY 12: WHEN AUTHORS WERE TORTURED

The moment the majority decides to destroy people for engaging in thought it dislikes, thought crime becomes a reality.

~ Ben Shapiro ~

Freedom of speech is taken for granted in most of the world, but it could get you killed, even tortured, for most of human history. One example of such persecution happened on this day in 1593, when playwright Thomas Kyd was arrested and tortured for libel.

Kyd and others were arrested for supposedly posting libelous tracts about the English government. Kyd accused his roommate, the more famous Christopher Marlowe, of owning blasphemous writings found in their quarters. In suspicious and still murky circumstances, Marlowe was murdered.

THOUGHT FOR TODAY: While writers rightly fear libel if they publish untrue and malicious content, they need not fear torture and death. Around the world today the freedom of the press is being challenged, but in most places the press remains free and independent.

MAY 13: DR. PAPANICOLAOU AND CANCER SCREENING

Cancer is a word, not a sentence.

~ John Diamond ~

Until recent decades, cancer was a death sentence. Both Hippocrates and Galen thought that there was little a doctor could do to halt its inexorable spread. Around the mid-1800s, with the dawn of surgical anesthesia, doctors could successfully remove internal tumors

Once surgical removal of tumors was practicable, doctors searched for ways to diagnose cancer early when cells were small. Dr. Georgios Papanicolaou, born on this day in 1883, studied vaginal fluid under a microscope and found cancerous cells in women who had cervical cancer. Another doctor used these findings to develop the Papanicolaou or "Pap" smear test.

THOUGHT FOR TODAY: Today there are many kinds of cancer screenings—biopsies, colonoscopes, blood tests—that save the lives of people living with cancer. Thanks to the march of medical science, cancer may someday be a thing of the past.

MAY 14: ISRAEL BECOMES A COUNTRY

Israel will endure and flourish. It is the child of hope and the home of the brave. It can neither be broken by adversity nor demoralized by success.

~ John F. Kennedy ~

Few religions have been as persecuted as much as Judaism. Jews were enslaved by the Egyptians, kidnapped by the Babylonians, ruled by the Persians, persecuted by the Greeks, and scattered by the Romans. They fared little better in Europe, where they were ghettoed and then gassed. When Israel was declared a state, Jews in Muslim majority Middle Eastern countries killed or expelled most of them. Since 1948, Israel has survived despite external invasion and internal insurrection.

 **THOUGHT FOR TODAY:** Israel's treatment of Palestinians is controversial, but the existence of a Jewish state to ensure the survival of the children of Abraham is a hopeful reminder of human resilience. In Israel, Jews practice their faith free of the persecution that preceded the foundation of the Jewish state.

MAY 15: EDWARD JENNER SAVES MILLIONS OF LIVES

I hope that someday the practice of producing cowpox in human beings will spread over the world - when that day comes, there will be no more smallpox.

~ Edward Jenner ~

Until the last two centuries, there were few effective strategies for preventing infectious diseases. In Constantinople and other places, people made the important insight that a small exposure to a disease might prevent it. Others observed that milkmaids, having been exposed to cowpox, rarely got sick from it. Variolation, a precursor to vaccination, was practiced in the 1700s with uncertain success.

Edward Jenner, an English doctor and scientist who was born this month in 1749, vaccinated his first patient on May 14, 1796. He subsequently tested his vaccine and proved that it prevented infection. Vaccination for disease prevention was born.

THOUGHT FOR TODAY: Jenner's work led to the eradication of smallpox, which used to kill millions. Child mortality has dropped precipitously because vaccines prevent childhood death from polio, measles, mumps, rubella and other pathogens.

MAY 16: LASERS COME TO LIGHT

We have grown accustomed to the wonders of clean water, indoor plumbing, laser surgery, artificial joints, and the much longer lives that accompany them.

~ S. Jay Olshansky ~

Blasting energy beams emanating from space ships or hand-held blasters have long been the stuff of science fiction. On this day in 1960, Theodore Maiman made sci-fi a reality with the first successful laser test at the Hughes Research Laboratory in California.

In the few decades since Maiman's discovery, laser innovations have proliferated. They are used in in bar code scanners, fiber-optic communications, printing, and measuring the speed of cars. Lasers are used in surgery and skin treatments as well as factory floors and makerspaces.

THOUGHT FOR TODAY: Back in 1960, it would have been hard to imagine all the applications that the laser would be used for. Today it is hard to imagine life without lasers. They make life safer, healthier and more enjoyable.

MAY 17: BROWN VS. BOARD OF EDUCATION TACKLES SEGREGATION

To separate them from others solely because of their race generates a feeling of inferiority as to their status in the community.

~ Chief Justice Earl Warren ~

On this day in 1954, the Supreme Court handed down their decision on *Brown v. Board of Education*. The high court determined that segregated facilities were unconstitutional because they denied citizens equal protection. This accelerated the Civil Rights movement as well as resistance by white majority governments in the South and other regions of the United States.

THOUGHT FOR TODAY: Denial of services due to race, let alone forced segregation, seem unthinkable today. Although issues of racial inequality still dog the United States, the conflicts are not as violent, nor as fundamental, as they were in the 1950s and 60s. The arc of the moral universe has slowly bent toward justice, including integration and equal rights.

MAY 18: A SIMPLE MEDICAL INSIGHT SAVES MILLIONS OF LIVES

Beauty commonly produces love, but cleanliness preserves it.

~ Joseph Addison ~

Until recent times, nearly all births occurred at home. Obstetric hospitals were established to prevent the infanticide of children born by sex workers or out of wedlock. These hospitals were the training grounds of obstetricians and nurses. Ignaz Semmelweis was one such doctor, and he noticed that the mortality rates between two birth clinics differed significantly. After a careful process of elimination, he realized that the clinic with the higher mortality rates was a place where medical students were also handling cadavers. This insight led to the development of germ theory...and meticulous hand washing of doctors as they moved between patients.

 **THOUGHT FOR TODAY:** Today most people die of diseases of old age because we have conquered many contagious diseases. This all began with Semmelweis' discovery of germ theory inferred after painstaking observation.

MAY 19: JOHNS HOPKINS, A NEW KIND OF AMERICAN UNIVERSITY

It's the best time ever to be a doctor because you can heal and treat conditions that were untreatable even a few years ago.

~ Joseph Murray ~

Johns Hopkins was a Maryland Quaker who pursued the American dream. His family emancipated their slaves in 1807. As a young man Hopkins received a free education and moved from his rural family plantation to Baltimore. He made his fortune by investing in the Baltimore and Ohio Railroad and became one of the richest men in America.

Hopkins, like Rockefeller and Carnegie, decided to give most of his wealth to philanthropic pursuits. His bequest formed the seed money of a Baltimore university, Johns Hopkins, which became one of the greatest medical colleges in the world.

THOUGHT FOR TODAY: Hopkins' bequest that founded the university and medical school made a difference that is still felt. Johns Hopkins Medical School pioneered the medical training residency, the first school of public health, antiseptic surgery, and other breakthroughs central to medical care.

MAY 20: THE BIRTH OF MODERN PHILANTHROPY

Never respect men merely for their riches, but rather for their philanthropy; we do not value the sun for its height, but for its use.

~ Gamaliel Bailey ~

Stephen Girard, born on this day in 1750, lived a rags to riches success story. He was born in France but settled in Philadelphia, where he started a shipping business that made him rich. After making this fortune, Girard bought most of the shares of the Bank of the United States and more than once kept the US solvent, which he considered acts of patriotism.

He lived a long, successful life, and when he died a legal battle broke out over his inheritance. The Supreme Court ruled in favor of Girard's philanthropic bequest, not his relatives, which established the right of donor intent.

THOUGHT FOR TODAY: Philanthropy—literally "love of humanity"—has grown in the most recent centuries. The largest of all, the Bill and Melinda Gates Foundation, has saved millions of lives through its health initiatives.

MAY 21: UN DAY FOR DIVERSITY, DIALOGUE AND DEVELOPMENT

A multicultural society does not reject the culture of the other but is prepared to listen, to dialogue and accept the other's culture without compromising its own.

~ Reuven Rivlin ~

For most of history, dominant cultures crushed the traditions of the conquered. In the United States, immigrants were expected to adopt the cultural attitudes and values dominant in America. In recent decades, multiculturalism has led to the celebration of all cultures. Children of immigrants who were encouraged not to speak their native tongues in America are flocking to language schools, joining cultural associations, and studying their genealogy.

THOUGHT FOR TODAY: The embrace of multiculturalism has been resisted by some, but social scientists are increasingly finding that diverse teams and workplaces produce more innovative ideas, a key for success in the 21st century. When you walk down the street of a modern metropolis like New York, New Delhi, or Nairobi, savor and celebrate the diversity.

MAY 22: THE MAYOR OF CASTRO STREET

If a bullet should enter my brain, let that bullet destroy every closet door.

~ Harvey Milk ~

Gay activist and martyr Harvey Milk was born on this day in 1930. Milk was closeted through his 40s, when he became active in local politics. He was an organizer who became known as "The Mayor of Castro Street," the heart of gay San Francisco. He ran for office unsuccessfully three times before he was elected to the city Board of Supervisors. While there, Milk led the passage of a strong gay rights ordinance. Less than a full year into his term, Milk and Mayor George Moscone were assassinated by a disgruntled Supervisor, Dan White.

THOUGHT FOR TODAY: Harvey Milk was the only prominent gay US politician in the late 1970s, but today LGBT Americans are prominent at all levels of business, entertainment and government.

MAY 23: THE FIRST FINGERPRINT CONVICTION

Many police departments use DNA evidence the way they have used fingerprints and tire tracks: to determine whether a suspect committed the crime.

~ Bill Dedman ~

Crime has paid for much of history because evidence for conviction was hard to find. One breakthrough was the invention of fingerprinting. In the 1800s criminologists studied the marks left by fingers and other body parts on smooth surfaces and discovered that these impressions were nearly unique to each individual.

On this day in 1905, the Stratton brothers were executed for murder of a husband and wife in Deptford, London. Fingerprint evidence found on the scene proved that the men were the murderers, and the case established the efficacy of this new crime fighting tool.

THOUGHT FOR TODAY: Advances in forensic sciences, from fingerprinting to DNA analysis, have made it harder for criminals to escape arrest and conviction. These improvements have made our era the safest in human history.

MAY 24: THE BROOKLYN BRIDGE SPANS THE EAST RIVER

Everyone should walk across the Brooklyn Bridge. I did it three days in a row because it was one of the most exhilarating experiences I've ever had.

~ Seann William Scott ~

On this day in 1883, one of the great engineering triumphs of the 19th century opened for traffic: The Brooklyn Bridge. At the time of its construction, it was the only land connection to between Brooklyn and Manhattan. The suspension design was relatively novel at the time. Its construction presaged the many bridges and tunnels that would connect the boroughs of New York, and cities around the world would use the various new bridge designs to connect across waterways that had previously served as barriers.

THOUGHT FOR TODAY: We are connected locally, nationally, and internationally more than ever. Some of those connections, like bridges, span physical barriers. Telephonic and internet connections mean that anyone can communicate with anyone anywhere in the world.

MAY 25: RINDERPEST ERADICATED

As medical research continues, and technology enables new breakthroughs, there will be a day when malaria and most major deadly diseases are eradicated on Earth.

~ Peter Diamandis ~

On this day in 2011, the World Organisation for Animal Health declared that rinderpest had been eradicated. Also known as cattle plague, rinderpest was the first animal disease ever to be wiped out. It caused fever, oral sores, diarrhea and eventually death in the cattle and buffalo that it affected. Rinderpest and smallpox are the only two diseases that have been eradicated, but we are close to wiping out polio, dracunculiasis (guinea worm), and efforts are underway to eliminate malaria, hookworm, measles, and rubella.

THOUGHT FOR TODAY: Until recently, humanity lived under the constant shadow of infectious disease. In the 20th century improvements in public health, especially vaccines and the treatment of diseases, has meant the eradication of some diseases and the near-elimination of others.

MAY 26: ROBERT HEINRICH HERMANN KOCH

If my efforts have led to greater success, this is due to the fact that during my wanderings, I have strayed onto paths where the gold was still lying by the wayside.

~ Robert Koch ~

Robert Koch was a German scientist who founded modern bacteriology. He pioneered the growth of bacterial cultures in agar mediums (those petri dishes with a thin layer of gelatin). Koch also found the cause of anthrax, tuberculosis, and cholera, work that helped subsequent scientists understand infectious diseases.

While he was in New Guinea, Koch took blood samples from natives and found that they had the malaria microorganisms in their bloodstream, yet they did not get nearly as sick from malaria as Europeans. From this insight he developed the theory of acquired immunity.

THOUGHT FOR TODAY: Robert Koch, who died in late May 1910, furthered the understanding of microbiology that helped understand disease vectors and improve public health. Following generations of scientists would discover treatments to treat bacteriological diseases, diseases that kill fewer and fewer people each year.

MAY 27: SILENT SPRING

I shall stick to my resolution of writing always what I think no matter whom it offends.

~ Julia Ward Howe ~

Rachel Carson's book *Silent Spring* documented, in powerful writing, the damage that DDT did to wildlife. In the wake of the book's publication, DDT was banned in the US and many other countries. In subsequent years populations of birds of prey, including the bald eagle and peregrine falcon, rebounded. Carson marshaled scientific evidence and explicated her argument in lovely prose.

THOUGHT FOR TODAY: When you a hawk, eagle or other large bird of prey soaring above you, thank Rachel Carson. In most of the world, raptor species were in sharp decline before Carson's Silent Spring alerted the world to the dangers of DDT on wildlife. Carson's work led to limitations on the use of DDT. The bald eagle, once at the brink of extinction, is abundant again thanks to the DDT ban inspired by Silent Spring.

MAY 28: SIERRA CLUB ESTABLISHED

Keep close to Nature's heart and break clear away, once in a while, and climb a mountain or spend a week in the woods. Wash your spirit clean.

~ John Muir ~

On this day in 1892, the Sierra Club was founded as a conservation organization. Its philosophical muse and founder, John Muir, was elected the first president. For their first action, the Sierra Club successfully lobbied against a proposed reduction in the size of Yosemite National Park. Today the Sierra Club has more than three million members and is a powerful voice for the environment and outdoor recreation.

THOUGHT FOR TODAY: In the 1800s, environmental awareness sprouted into a few organizations and movements. Today there are thousands of environmental organizations around the world with millions of members. While many critical environmental problems need to be solved, the environmental movement is a powerful global force for the protection of the earth, thanks in part to the Sierra Club.

MAY 29: HILLARY AND NORGAY REACH THE HIGHEST HIGH

You don't have to be a hero to accomplish great things—to compete. You can just be an ordinary chap, sufficiently motivated to reach challenging goals.

~ Edmund Hillary ~

On May 29, 1953, Edmund Hillary and Tensing Norgay became the first climbers to summit Mount Everest, the world's highest peak. George Finch was the first to make a serious attempt at the peak in 1922, but it wasn't until 1953 that it was successfully summited. When Tensing and Hillary returned to camp, Hillary's first words to the trip's leader were "Well George, we've knocked the bastard off."

THOUGHT FOR TODAY: Climbing the highest peak in the world was long thought to be impossible, but people often do the impossible. The same strivings that drove Hillary and Tensing to the summit of Everest urged Beethoven to write symphonies, Edison to invent the lightbulb, and Watson and Crick to unravel the mysteries of life.

MAY 30: BETTER SURGERY

> The damage that the human body can survive these days is as awesome as it is horrible: a ruptured colon, a massive heart attack, rampaging infection. These conditions had once been uniformly fatal.
>
> *~ Atul Gawande ~*

The history of surgery until modern times is grim reading. Without anesthesia, sterile instruments, and blood transfusions, survival rates from surgery were low. However, as these innovations became standard, survival rates increased and recovery times decreased.

One important milestone was the invention of thoracoscopic examination and surgery. The first thoracoscopes were first used in the mid-1800s. In 1910, Hans Christian Jacobaeus, who was born this month in 1879, made the first thoracoscopic diagnosis of tuberculosis.

THOUGHT FOR TODAY: Today millions of minimally invasive diagnostic procedures and surgeries are performed around the world, be they for gallbladder removal, knee surgery, or more serious heart operations. Minimally invasive surgery leads to less blood loss, better outcomes, and quicker recovery. Most recently, robots have been employed for surgery, and we can expect more innovations in the future.

MAY 31: NEREUS REACHES THE BOTTOM

Every time you dive, you hope you'll see something new - some new species. Sometimes the ocean gives you a gift, sometimes it doesn't.

~ James Cameron ~

Around the time that humans were first sending astronauts into space, we started plumbing the deepest reaches of the ocean. The first deep dive bathyscaphes were built after World War II. In 1960, the bathyscaphe *Trieste* dove more than 35,000 feet to the deepest part of the ocean in the Marianas Trench.

More recently, the *Nereus* has been prowling and probing the deepest depths of the ocean. On this day in 2009, the *Nereus* reached the Challenger Deep, the region of the Marianas Trench first explored by the *Trieste*.

THOUGHT FOR TODAY: Just as humans continue to probe the depths of space, so too do we explore the briny deep of the oceans. New insights further scientific understanding and often lead to practical solutions to environmental problems.

JUNE 1: WORLD CHILDREN'S DAY

Extremists have shown what frightens them the most: a girl with a book.

~ Malala Yousafzai ~

Today is World Children's Day, and there is much to celebrate. Throughout the world, rates of education have never been higher. In India, 99% of girls and 95% of boys attend primary school. According to *The National*, some 58,000 government schools and 70,700 private schools were built in India between 2009 and 2015.

The successes in India highlight what is happening in the developing world: more and more children, especially girls, are attending school. Until recently, families would spend limited resources on boys, and many girls were pulled out of school early to become wives. Not anymore.

THOUGHT FOR TODAY: Throughout the world, girls are attending primary school at rates nearly as high as boys. The dream of universal education—and equal rights and opportunities for men and women—is coming closer to reality.

JUNE 2: REGAL CORONATION BECOMES ENTERTAINMENT

Therefore, I am sure that this, my Coronation, is not the symbol of a power and splendor that are gone but a declaration of our hopes for the future.

~ Queen Elizabeth II ~

Throughout history, the coronation of monarchs were opportunities for states to inspire fear and awe. But by the middle of the 20th century, the power of royals around the world was waning.

On this day in 1952, Elizabeth was crowned Queen of England. It was the first time that TV was used to broadcast an event around the world. The historic telecast displayed to a global audience the decline of regal power and the advent of figurehead monarchs. As democracy gained ascendance, kings and queens became an expression of national pride and identity, not showcases of dynastic power.

THOUGHT FOR TODAY: In the 20th century, democracy supplanted monarchy as the most common form of government. The trend continues as political power expands to the people and rights go out to the formerly disempowered.

JUNE 3: LONG DISTANCE POWER

We forget how painfully dim the world was before electricity. A candle provides barely a hundredth of the illumination of a single 100-watt light bulb.

~ Bill Bryson ~

Electricity has changed life in innumerable ways. It brings light, heat and power to homes and businesses. A step toward powering the planet happened on this day in in 1889, when the first long-distance electric power transmission line in the United States was put into operation. In the late 1800s and early 1900s, cities developed electric power infrastructure and life was transformed...and illuminated.

For those who think that electric power is a luxury, visit a slum in a developing country and look at the ingenious infrastructure of "pirated" power that slum dwellers create. The poor want power because it replaces wood and dung for cooking, the exhaust of which kills more than a million people each year.

THOUGHT FOR TODAY: Ubiquitous electric power has made the world safer, less polluted, and life much more convenient.

JUNE 4: INSTITUT PASTEUR FOUNDED

In the field of observation, chance favors the prepared mind.

~ Louis Pasteur ~

Louis Pasteur's list of accomplishments would be enough for five august scientists. His achievements prevented countless deaths, saved industries, and advanced science. His greatest legacy may be his Institut Pasteur, which was founded on this day in 1887. The Institut did important work in fighting infectious diseases, especially diphtheria, tetanus, tuberculosis, polio, flu, yellow fever and HIV. Since 1900, Institut Pasteur scientists have been awarded a whopping ten Nobel Prizes.

THOUGHT FOR TODAY: Institutions of higher learning and scientific research have become more abundant and effective in exploring and solving big problems. From the Royal Society to Bell Labs and the Max Planck Institute, research institutions are engines of human progress and increase our well-being.

JUNE 5: THE POWER OF THE PEN

So you are the little woman who wrote the book that started this great war!

~ Abraham Lincoln to Harriet Beecher Stowe ~

Widespread literacy has changed the world in many ways. Gutenberg's printing press increased the number of books and encouraged literacy. During the Enlightenment, the novel developed as an important form of entertainment, and many of these books changed the course of history.

Such was the case with Harriet Beecher Stowe's anti-slavery book *Uncle Tom's Cabin*, which began its publication as a serialized novel on this day in 1851. Stowe's novel is cited as a cause of the Civil War, the conflict that ended slavery in America.

THOUGHT FOR TODAY: In 1800, only 12% of the population was literate. Today, according to Our World in Data, more than four out of five people can read. And thanks to widespread literacy, novels like Uncle Tom's Cabin changed minds and changed the world. The power of the pen is mighty indeed!

JUNE 6: YMCA FOUNDED

Living in the YMCA in Harlem dramatically broadened my view of the world.

~ Constance Baker Motley ~

In the 1800s, industrialization swept through the United States, which caused young people to migrate from rural to urban areas in search of work. Fearing the satanic mills and city life would ruin the rustic purity of rural youngsters, the Young Men's Christian Association (YMCA) was started on June 6, 1844. It "established...a safe Christian environment for rural young men... journeying to the cities."

Today YMCAs are known as local recreation centers that support the health and well-being of *all* people. Currently, 9 million youths and 13 million adults in the US belong to some 2700 YMCAs.

THOUGHT FOR TODAY: Organizations like the YMCA often begin with a specific mission for specific people that later broadens to serve all people. This spirit of community development has made the social fabric of America stronger.

JUNE 7: THE PILL BECOMES AVAILABLE TO ALL

> In my opinion, the battles over birth control and Planned Parenthood are primarily neither political nor religious. This is an issue of equality for women.
>
> *~ Karen DeCrow ~*

On June 7, 1965, the Supreme Court ruled 7-2 in Griswold v. Connecticut that women are free to obtain birth control pills because of a right to marital privacy. For most of history, women's reproductive decisions were determined by men and circumscribed by society. With the development of the birth control pill in the late 1950s, women had a new tool to control reproduction and plan parenthood. It also allowed for increased sexual freedom.

 **THOUGHT FOR TODAY:** The right to effective contraception has given women more freedom and helped slow population growth. Women have gained many rights, especially in the last century, including the vote, legal independence, and the right to buy contraception. If past progress is a guide, full equality for women is a matter of when, not if.

JUNE 8: 1984 PUBLISHED

If liberty means anything at all, it means the right to tell people what they do not want to hear.

~ George Orwell ~

On this day in 1949, George Orwell's masterpiece *1984* was published. It described a drab totalitarian state where Big Brother wielded a relentless propaganda machine and perfected thought control. At the height of the Cold War, world conquest by totalitarian governments seemed possible.

Luckily, people were not as malleable as Orwell predicted. Despite attempts at thought control, most communist governments toppled circa 1990. While populism is surging in today's world, democracy continues to spread.

THOUGHT FOR TODAY: In the early 1950s, when Stalin ruled Russia and Mao commanded China, Orwell's dystopian vision of totalitarianism seemed likely. But totalitarianism failed. Russia and the US are no longer pointing missiles at each other, and countries rarely invade each other anymore. Death rates from war and all other kinds of violence are near historic lows.

JUNE 9: NO SENSE OF DECENCY?

No one man can terrorize a whole nation unless we are all his accomplices

~ Edward R. Murrow ~

The 1950s, despite its reputation as a golden age in America, was a fearful time. The Cold War often ran hot, especially during the Korean War, U2 crisis, and Sputnik launch. One of the worst episodes was Joseph McCarthy's witch hunt against suspected communists.

On this day in 1954, McCarthy was grilling Joseph Welch, to which Welch famously replied, "At long last, have you left no sense of decency?" This challenge, televised on TV, broke the senator's hypnotic hold on America. McCarthy was eventually censured by his Senate peers.

THOUGHT FOR TODAY: Political witch hunts happen, but democracy has a way of biting back. McCarthy was the most feared man of Washington until he was confronted, at which point he fell from power. Despite their frightening power, populists like McCarthy are often undone by their own excesses.

JUNE 10: EQUAL PAY FOR EQUAL WORK

Feminism isn't about making women strong. Women are already strong.

~ G.D. Anderson ~

For much of the 20th century, discrimination against women was a persistent problem. Women did not even gain the right to vote in national elections in the US until 1920. When Member of Congress Winifred Stanley proposed in the early 1940s that women get equal pay for equal work, her bill was rebuffed. Little was done until President Kennedy signed the Equal Pay Act on this day in 1963.

THOUGHT FOR TODAY: While the wage gap between women and men still exists, it continues to get smaller. In 2017 Iceland passed a law that demanded employers prove that women receive equal pay for equal work. Women have given up the corset and round-the-clock domestic drudgery for school, college, career...and freedom.

JUNE 11: HELPING THE BODY TO FIGHT CANCER

Cancer is not a death sentence, but rather it is a life sentence; it pushes one to live.

~ Marcia Smith ~

After World War II, chemotherapy was developed as a treatment to destroy cancer cells. Unfortunately, most chemotherapy treatments are toxic to the whole body, not just the cancer cells. On this day in 1968, Lloyd J. Old identified cell antigens that were important first findings in the field of cancer immunotherapy. Today scientists are developing immunotherapy techniques with an aim to cure all cancers.

THOUGHT FOR TODAY: Cancer, once seen as a death sentence, is being effectively combatted by many research and treatment breakthroughs. Immunotherapy leverages the body's natural disease fighting agents to battle one of modernity's top killers. Just as smallpox, polio and TB were thought to be invulnerable—but were eliminated or controlled—cancer will be conquered and become a thing of the past.

JUNE 12: A LOVING DECISION

I am proud that Richard's and my name is on a court case that can help reinforce the love that so many people, black or white, young or old, gay or straight seek in life.

~ Mildred Loving ~

Slavery in America did not begin as a race-based institution, but it became one in by the late 1600s. Slavery and indentured servitude could befall Europeans, Indians and Africans alike, but by 1700, nearly all of the enslaved people in North America were African or the descendants of Africans.

Even after slavery was abolished after the Civil War, laws and customs forbade the marriage of blacks and whites. A biracial couple, Mildred and Richard Loving, violated Virginia's Racial Integrity Law when the married. On this day in 1967, the Supreme Court struck down all laws banning interracial marriage.

THOUGHT FOR TODAY: The Loving v. Virginia decision was another stepping stone in undoing the American tragedy of slavery and discrimination against blacks.

JUNE 13: RIGHTS OF THE ACCUSED

You have the right to remain silent. Anything you say can be used against you in a court of law.

~ The Miranda Rights ~

In the movie *Casablanca*, Claude Rains tells his police underlings to "round up the usual suspects" to cover up the murder of a Nazi officer. Sadly, much of the history of policing was similarly unprofessional and self-serving. While the Founding Fathers put protections for the accused in the US Constitution, many Americans were not educated about their guaranteed protections.

On this day in 1966, the Supreme Court ruled in *Miranda v. Arizona* that police must inform suspects of their Constitutional rights.

THOUGHT FOR TODAY: The expansion of the rule of law and high standards of conduct for police and public officials have played a part in the historic decrease in crime. Professionalization of policing makes our society safer and protects the strong and weak alike.

JUNE 14: THE FATHER OF TRANSFUSION MEDICINE

Prior to penicillin and medical research, death was an everyday occurrence. It was intimate.

~ Katherine Dunn ~

People have long recognized that blood was crucial to life. In the early 1800s, some doctors tried to transfuse blood from one person to another to save the recipient's life, but the recipient died because their body rejected the blood. Karl Landsteiner, who was born this day in 1868, made discoveries that would allow for successful blood transfusions. Landsteiner found that there were several blood types and that a recipient's type must match the donor's.

THOUGHT FOR TODAY: Many discrete discoveries have been made in the last 200 years of medical history that transformed our lives for the better. Blood transfusions meant that massive blood loss did not mean certain death. Additionally, life-saving surgeries became much more successful when patients' blood loss could be replenished through blood transfusions.

JUNE 15: A GREAT CHARTER THAT LIMITS KINGLY POWER

Here is a law which is above the King and which even he must not break.

~ Winston Churchill ~

On this day in 1215, a group of English barons limited the powers of King John at Runnymede. Magna Carta, or "Great Charter," was signed by the King of England. It sought to limit cruel punishments, guarantee trials by juries of peers, and that justice should be done expeditiously, among other rights.

THOUGHT FOR TODAY: Magna Carta was the foundation of rule of law in England and the countries it would later rule. Monarchies were accustomed to unchecked power. Over the next centuries, the power of English kings would slowly be circumscribed and then sundered to the rule of the people.

JUNE 16: JOHN SNOW'S PUBLIC HEALTH INSIGHT

I loved clinical practice, but in public health, the whole society is your patient.

~ Tom Frieden ~

In the early 1800s, people thought that foul air was the cause of infectious disease. During the London cholera epidemic of 1854, John Snow, who died on this day in 1858, decided to find the cause of the outbreak. With the help of Reverend Henry Whitehead, Snow talked to local residents and determined that the source of the spread of cholera was the public water pump on Broad Street. After local government officials closed the well, Snow created a dot map of cholera cases and applied statistical methods to determine the source of diseased water.

THOUGHT FOR TODAY: Snow's sleuthing during the 1854 cholera outbreak birthed the field of epidemiology and advanced public health. Today many diseases, cholera among them, have been stamped out in places with clean water, sewage and public health regulations.

JUNE 17: EAT YOUR VEGETABLES DAY

The more colorful the food, the better. I try to add color to my diet, which means vegetables and fruits.

~ Misty May-Treanor ~

Thanks to an overabundance of high calorie foods, children avoid vegetables. To encourage youngsters to eat healthier, June 17 is Eat Your Vegetables Day.

It would be easy to think that civilization has hit another low when healthy food needs to be encouraged. What it really shows is how abundant food has become. In the 1970s, dystopian books like *The Population Bomb* and *Famine 1975!* argued that overpopulation would lead to massive famines. Instead, progress has led to another epidemic—obesity.

 **THOUGHT FOR TODAY:** While obesity is a major problem, malnutrition is much worse. Malnutrition most severely affects young people and damages them for a lifetime. We need to make sure that people today eat right and exercise, but the fact that we have enough food to feed everyone is an achievement to celebrate.

JUNE 18: BIRTH OF A MALARIA PIONEER

There will be statues of Bill Gates across the Third World. There's a reasonable shot that - because of his money - we will cure malaria.

~ Malcolm Gladwell ~

Charles Louis Alphonse Laveran was born this day in 1845. He worked as a doctor for the French military during and after the Franco-Prussian War. After that, he worked in Algeria, where he discovered the Plasmodium protozoan that caused malaria, and the Trypanosoma that caused African Sleeping Sickness.

In the subsequent century, preventative measures and treatments have been developed to fight malaria, and Suramin has been developed to treat African Sleeping Sickness and River Blindness.

Laveran was awarded the Nobel Prize in 1907 for his work in discovering the protozoans that cause malaria and sleeping sickness.

THOUGHT FOR TODAY: With the advance of science, more and more diseases are treatable, and fewer people are dying from communicable diseases.

JUNE 19: LEGAL REPRESENTATION FOR THE POOR

Each era finds an improvement in law for the benefit of mankind.

~ Clarence Earl Gideon ~

The US Constitution guarantees the right to the assistance of an attorney in criminal cases. But legal counsel is expensive, and many poor defendants cannot afford lawyers. Gideon v. Wainwright changed this. Clarence Earl Gideon was convicted of breaking into a pool hall. He wrote letters from his cell to the Supreme Court stating that the Constitution guaranteed his right to a court-appointed attorney. Gideon's letters were answered, and his case eventually went to the Supreme Court, who appointed future Supreme Court justice Abe Fortas (whose birthday is June 19) to represent him. The Supreme Court unanimously ruled in his favor.

THOUGHT FOR TODAY: The Gideon decision led to the creation of a widespread public defender service throughout the United States. Thanks to Gideon, all people accused of a crime can count on legal representation.

JUNE 20: CROSSING THE ATLANTIC UNDER STEAM

For my part, I travel not to go anywhere, but to go. The great affair is to move.

~ Robert Louis Stevenson ~

Five hundred years ago, the most daring explorers were just starting to cross wide oceans. Within a hundred years, merchants and settlers were crisscrossing the world's seas. And on this date in 1819, the *SS Savannah* was the first steam-propelled vessel to cross the Atlantic Ocean. Today thousands of ships are transporting billions of tons of cargo around the world in a global network of trade. And now few people travel by ship to cross oceans. Airplanes take about 8 million passengers aloft each day.

THOUGHT FOR TODAY: No one could have predicted the progress of transport in the last 500 years. World travel, once the provenance of the "jet set," is now unremarkable. Governments and entrepreneurs are exploring opportunities for space travel. Who knows where we'll end up!

JUNE 21: THE G.I. BILL OPENS COLLEGE TO A NEW GENERATION

The goal after the war should be the maximum utilization of our human and material resources.

~ Franklin Roosevelt ~

At the height of World War II, the Servicemen's Readjustment Act of 1944, better known as the G.I. Bill, made its way through Congress and was signed by President Franklin Roosevelt. The revolutionary legislation swung into action when the troops started coming home in 1945. Within ten years, millions of veterans used G.I. Bill benefits to get help with mortgages, job training, and college education. Before World War II, universities were the province of a small minority of Americans. With the G.I. Bill, a better-educated workforce fueled America's explosive postwar economic growth.

THOUGHT FOR TODAY: Before the G.I. Bill, universities were elite institutions beyond the reach of most Americans. Today, thanks in part to the growth that the G.I. Bill encouraged, most American adults have some tertiary education, and university degree attainment rates continue to rise.

JUNE 22: SMOKE ON THE WATER

Cleveland, even now I can remember

'Cause the Cuyahoga River

Goes smokin' through my dreams

~ *Lyrics from "Burn On" by Randy Newman* ~

On this day in 1969, the Cuyahoga River in Cleveland, Ohio burned. It burned because for more than 100 years humans had been dumping waste directly into waterways. The Clean Water Act in 1972 led to significant improvements in water quality, a trend followed around the world. For example, for hundreds of years the Thames River was treated as a sewer and was pronounced "biologically dead" in 1957. Because of cleanup efforts, the river is the home to cormorants, seals and whales.

THOUGHT FOR TODAY: Many people seem to think that the earth has never been more polluted, but things were much worse in the 19th and 20th centuries, where rivers were polluted with human and industrial waste, and the sky was full of black smoke from home heating fires and the factories of the early industrial revolution.

JUNE 23: TITLE IX

Nobody goes undefeated all the time. If you can pick up after a crushing defeat, and go on to win again, you are going to be a champion someday.

~ Wilma Rudolph ~

Title IX is a federal law that prohibits discrimination on the basis of sex in any educational program or activity that receives federal funding. On this day in 1972 it was signed by President Nixon and became law. Title IX has been controversial because it may have led to the curtailing of collegiate men's athletic programs, but it has undoubtedly led to the proliferation of women's programs. In the 45 years since its inception, sports participation in schools by girls and women has increased tenfold.

THOUGHT FOR TODAY: Despite imperfect attempts at increasing equality, Title IX and other programs have encouraged females to participate in activities, such as sports, that were once dominated by males.

JUNE 24: SWIFT'S METHOD OF SLOWING THE ROT

Don't let the best you have done so far be the standard for the rest of your life.

~ Gustavus Franklin Swift ~

Meat rots. For this reason, early humans feasted on it right after the kill. Later we learned to salt, smoke and jerk meat to slow the rot. Gustavus Franklin Swift, who was born on this day in 1839, was keen to find a way to transport meat via rail in ways that prevented spoilage. Working with Andrew Chase in 1878, Swift designed a car that solved the considerable challenges. Swift & Company ushered in the age of refrigerated food transport.

THOUGHT FOR TODAY: Food waste and spoilage have always bedeviled humans. With the invention of refrigerated transport, perishable food could be transported year round. The development of the refrigerated freight car is one of many reasons why humans have more food per capita today than at any other time in history.

JUNE 25: THE ELIMINATE PROJECT TAKES ON TETANUS

True security is based on people's welfare - on a thriving economy, on strong public health and education programmes.

~ Ban Ki-moon ~

Maternal and neonatal tetanus kills more than 50,000 children a year. Nonetheless, this number is 85% lower than it was in 1990. On this day in 2010, Kiwanis International partnered with UNICEF with a goal to eliminate maternal and neonatal tetanus globally. Improvements have been significant, and through continuing efforts, these organizations hope to end maternal and neonatal tetanus.

THOUGHT FOR TODAY: We live in an era where giant service organizations work together to eliminate diseases like polio, malaria, guinea worm and tetanus. Thanks to simple public health interventions, billions of deaths have been prevented. For example, according to the World Health Organization, between 1980 and 2016, global cases of tetanus fell from 2 million to less than 200,000, a decrease of 1.8 million cases.

JUNE 26: EVERYONE GAINS THE RIGHT TO MARRY

Today's ruling from the Supreme Court affirms what millions across the country already know to be true in our hearts: that our love is equal.

~ James Obergefell ~

On the 26th of June, 2015, the Supreme Court legalized same sex marriage in the United States. While acceptance of gay marriage had been increasing in the early years of the 21st century, the ruling by the high court settled the issue for the time being. Since the 2015 ruling, gay marriage has expanded in Colombia, Germany, Malta, Finland and Australia.

 **THOUGHT FOR TODAY:** For most of human history, only a few wealthy, powerful—and straight—males had full rights. Thanks to Enlightenment ideas about universal rights—and the hard work of reformers—we are moving toward a future where all people have the same basic rights.

JUNE 27: NEW CLEAN ENERGY

We must learn to set our emotions aside and embrace what science tells us. GMOs and nuclear power are two of the most effective green technologies we have.

~ Ramez Naam ~

Ever since cavemen roasted woolly mammoth on open fires, people have used wood to create heat and light. More recently, coal and then petroleum were exploited as cleaner, more efficient energy sources. Now we can use water, wind and solar power to generate electricity. The cleanest, most powerful—and most controversial—source to generate electricity debuted in late June of 1954: nuclear power. The Obninsk Nuclear Power Plant opened, and since then hundreds of nuclear plants have gone online to produce much of the world's power with virtually no pollutants or carbon emissions.

 **THOUGHT FOR TODAY:** Judging by lives lost per units of energy output, nuclear power is the safest and cleanest energy source. In this era of global warming, irrational prejudice against nuclear power needs to be overcome before we can fully utilize this amazing energy source.

JUNE 28: STONEWALL RIOTS BEGIN

Whether it's Lincoln and the Emancipation Proclamation or gay rights, I think there is an almost-inevitable march toward greater civil liberties.

~ James McGreevey ~

Gays have been subject to persecution since the beginning of time. Some brave individuals and groups stood up to this persecution, but most were cowed by virulent homophobia. On this day in 1969, the police raided the Stonewall Inn bar in New York City. This time, the persecuted fought back in what became a touchstone event in the struggle for LGBT rights. In the wake of the Stonewall Riots, new gay rights organizations formed, and the equal rights movement was energized.

THOUGHT FOR TODAY: While LGBT people are still denied rights and protections, there has been a great deal of progress since Stonewall. In 2016, President Obama established Stonewall National Monument to honor Stonewall's place in American history. Today, gay pride marches and celebrations occur around the world every June to commemorate the progress made since 1969.

JUNE 29: TESLA GOES PUBLIC

When Henry Ford made cheap, reliable cars people said, "Nah, what's wrong with a horse?" That was a huge bet he made, and it worked.

~ Elon Musk ~

Until the late 1800s, horses were the prime movers of people around cities. With the invention of the internal combustion engine, automobiles replaced horse-powered transport. The car led to the reduction in one of the most noxious emissions of all: horse manure. Over the decades, automobile emissions have been reduced by innovations like lead-free gasoline and catalytic converters. Today, the newest anti-pollution innovation—the electric car—is becoming more and more common on our streets.

On this day in 2010, Tesla, founded by billionaire Elon Musk, made his electric car company the first American automotive IPO since Ford went public in 1956.

 **THOUGHT FOR TODAY:** Thanks to innovations, transport is safer, cheaper, cleaner and more abundant. In recent times countries have committed to a future of zero-emissions automobiles, which will lead to cleaner air and a cleaner planet.

JUNE 30: LIFESAVING LAWS

Regulation is necessary to protect our natural environment, keep our food and medicine safe, and ensure fair competition and fair treatment of our workers.

~ Marco Rubio ~

Upton Sinclair, in his famous exposé, *The Jungle*, brought the unregulated meat packing industry into the national spotlight. Soon after the book's publication, President Theodore Roosevelt commissioned a study of the meatpacking industry. The commission discovered firsthand the unsanitary conditions in the factories, which convinced Roosevelt to sign the Meat Inspection Act. The new law, signed on this day in 1906, mandated inspection of livestock before and after slaughter, and ongoing monitoring and inspection of slaughter and processing operations.

THOUGHT FOR TODAY: Government regulation is often dismissed as bad for business, but common-sense regulations like the Meat Inspection Act ensure quality and good health. Additionally, the USDA seal of approval builds confidence in the industry, which is good for business. Before decrying regulation outright, the many (mostly invisible) benefits must be considered.

JULY 1: CONGRESS ACCEPTS SMITHSON'S BEQUEST

James Smithson was well aware that knowledge should not be viewed as existing in isolated parts, but as a whole.

~ Joseph Henry ~

Founded "for the increase and diffusion of knowledge," the Smithsonian Institution was founded in 1846. It began with the bequest left by James Smithson, which Congress accepted on this day in 1836. The Smithsonian grew with the young nation into the world's largest museum, education and research institution with 19 museums, the National Zoo, and nine other research facilities.

Most of the Smithsonian museums are located along the National Mall in Washington, DC, nearly all of which are free and open to the public.

THOUGHT FOR TODAY: Museums were once the storehouses of the rich, and research institutions served the narrow interests of the upper crust. Today accessible organizations like the Smithsonian have proliferated, as has our understanding of history, culture and the natural world.

JULY 2: THE CIVIL RIGHTS ACT IS PASSED

The Civil Rights Act enshrined into law the basic principle upon which our country was founded: that all people are created equal.

~ Thomas E. Perez ~

Slavery and the mistreatment of Black Americans is a tragic theme of American history. The Civil War ended slavery but began an era of Jim Crow and separate but unequal citizenship for Black Americans. It wasn't until 99 years after the Civil War ended that federal law enshrined equal rights.

On this day in 1964, the Civil Rights Act was approved after surviving an 83-day filibuster in the Senate. It outlawed discrimination based on race, unequal application of voter eligibility requirements, and segregation.

THOUGHT FOR TODAY: Positive change had been too slow in civil rights, but it has been inevitable. Despite opposition, the civil rights of all minorities, be they racial minorities, children, or LGBT citizens, continue to expand. the US is moving closer to the ideal expressed in the Declaration of Independence, that all people are created equal.

JULY 3: THE SALVATION ARMY MARCHES

While little children go hungry, as they do now, I'll fight. While men go to prison, in and out, in and out, as they do now, I'll fight-I'll fight to the very end!

~ William Booth ~

In the 1800s, many reformers founded organizations to help the urban poor. One that is still going strong is the Salvation Army, which was founded in July 1865 in London. William Booth, a Methodist preacher, and his wife Catherine created the East London Christian Mission to meet the physical and spiritual needs of poor city dwellers.

It is still going strong today with some 1.5 million members, according to Salvation Army statistics. Today the Army is known for its brass bands, substance abuse centers, thrift shops, youth groups, and red kettle appeals during the December holidays.

THOUGHT FOR TODAY: Many community organizations exist to support the poor, the unemployed, and those recovering from addiction. Groups like the Salvation Army provide meaning for its members and lend a helping hand to those who need one.

JULY 4: THE DECLARATION OF INDEPENDENCE

We hold these truths to be self-evident, that all men are created equal.

~ The Declaration of Independence ~

Revolution was in the air in 1776, but it was an enlightened one. The Founding Fathers who wrote the Declaration of Independence were influenced by Enlightenment thinkers like Locke, Montesquieu, Rousseau and Voltaire.

One this day in 1776, the Continental Congress in Philadelphia signed the Declaration of Independence, a document that would provide the philosophical foundations of American government and inspire people around the world to work for democracy.

THOUGHT FOR TODAY: While the Declaration was an imperfect work—it did not lead to the freedom of Indians, enslaved African Americans, or women—it was a start. The hypocrisy of American ideals, so beautifully written by Jefferson in the Declaration, would spur generations of reformers to make America live up to its founding ideals.

JULY 5: THOMAS COOK BRINGS TRAVEL TO THE MASSES

Thomas Cook took travel from the privileged and gave it to the people.

~ Robert Runcie ~

Today, travel to foreign countries is considered a normal diversion of the middle class, but for most of history, only the very rich traveled for leisure. On this day in 1841, British tourism pioneer Thomas Cook led his first travel excursion from Leicester to Loughborough. In the subsequent decade Cook expanded his travel offerings until, in 1851, he arranged for 150,000 tourists to travel to the London Exposition. In 1872 he founded Thomas Cook & Son, the first global travel agency that still operates today.

THOUGHT FOR TODAY: Mark Twain summed up the benefits of travel well: "It is fatal to prejudice, bigotry and narrow-mindedness, and many of our people need it sorely on these accounts. Broad, wholesome, charitable views of men and things cannot be acquired by vegetating in one little corner of the earth all one's lifetime."

JULY 6: WHITE HATS OF THE INTERNET

The Electronic Frontier Foundation is the leading nonprofit organization defending civil liberties in the digital world.

~ Electronic Frontier Foundation ~

The growth of the internet has been a bit like the Wild West in the 1870s: The pioneers arrive before the law gets established. The Electronic Frontier Foundation (EFF) was formed on this day in 1990 to safeguard civil liberties on the internet. To this end, the organization is involved in many projects to keep the internet free, including its Transparency Project, which aims to watchdog government and expose diminishment of civil liberties. EFF lawyers use the Freedom of Information Act to shine a light on any potential government usurpation of rights.

THOUGHT FOR TODAY: During the industrial revolution, governments were slow to respond to the rapid changes that transformed society in so many good and bad ways. The EFF and organizations like it aim to quickly respond to the rapid changes brought on by technological change.

JULY 7: MOTHER JONES AND THE MILL MARCH

Someday the workers will take possession of your city hall, and when we do, no child will be sacrificed on the altar of profit!

~ Mother Jones ~

Mary Harris "Mother" Jones was an Irish-born American activist who championed labor causes and the rights of children. On this day in 1903, she led a march of child and adult textile laborers from Philadelphia to New York to publicize their plight. The march brought publicity to child labor and led to the creation of the National Child Labor Committee. In the following year, Pennsylvania tightened its child labor laws. Despite these successes, child labor protections weren't guaranteed until the Fair Labor Standards Act was enacted during the New Deal.

THOUGHT FOR TODAY: Today we consider childhood sacred. Young people are expected to be cared for and go to school. Thanks to the work of Mother Jones and many other reformers, the lot of children today is much better than it was 100 years ago.

JULY 8: MEASURING INTELLIGENCE

The function of education is to teach one to think intensively and to think critically. Intelligence plus character - that is the goal of true education.

~ Martin Luther King ~

Is intelligence an inborn or cultivated trait? Psychologist Alfred Binet, who was born this day in 1857, became interested in this question with the birth of his daughters, who seemed to have very different types of intellects. Later in his career he would create a test to determine if students needed remedial help in school.

This test was adapted in America as the Stanford-Binet test and is still used today. Psychological testing has improved greatly since Binet's first test, but he can be thanked for his pioneering work in the field of measuring intelligence.

THOUGHT FOR TODAY: Since Binet developed his test, education has improved and people have been getting smarter. Psychologist James Flynn has found that IQ test scores improve by a few points each decade, which means the children today will probably be the smartest generation yet.

JULY 9: OPEN HEART, BROKEN BARRIERS

Creative experimentation propels our culture forward. As any artist or scientist knows, without some protected space for mistakes, innovation would cease.

~ Evgeny Morozov ~

On this day in 1893, African-American doctor Daniel Hale Williams performed the second successful open-heart surgery in the United States. It was the first in the US to be performed without anesthesia, which makes the feat all the more astounding. Despite his prowess as a surgeon, Williams lived in a racist society that did not allow white and black medical professionals to work together, so he founded the first integrated hospital in the US, Provident Hospital in Chicago.

THOUGHT FOR TODAY: The success of Daniel Hale Williams reminds us of the progress we made in the 20th century. In the 21st century, deaths from heart disease have fallen sharply thanks to medical progress pioneered by doctors like Daniel Hale Williams.

JULY 10: A TURNING POINT FOR A TERRORIST GROUP

Choose your enemies carefully 'cos they will define you.

~ Bono, in the U2 song "Cedars of Lebanon" ~

Terrorism dominated politics and the headlines in the first years of the 21st century. But do terrorists win? Rarely.

The ETA organization fought for a separate Basque nation for more than 50 years. On this day in 1997, ETA terrorists kidnapped a local Spanish politician and demanded that Spain transfer ETA prisoners to prisons in the Basque region. When the government refused, Blanco was shot in the back of the head, an ETA trademark. Protests at this brutality ensued and support for ETA waned. In early 2017, ETA agreed to surrender their weapons.

THOUGHT FOR TODAY: Terrorism is a dead-end strategy that rarely works. For this reason, nations should take a cool-headed, long-term strategy because time is not on the side of the terrorists.

JULY 11: SCOUT, JEM, AND ATTICUS

You never really understand a person until you consider things from his point of view - until you climb into his skin and walk around in it.

*~ **Atticus Finch, in** To Kill a Mockingbird ~*

Sometimes a good story is more convincing that logical arguments. *Uncle Tom's Cabin* convinced its readers that slavery was barbaric. One hundred years after *Uncle Tom's Cabin*, Harper Lee wrote a novel about two siblings and their attorney father who defend a black man accused of raping a white woman. *To Kill a Mockingbird* gave white readers a window into the depravities of Jim Crow from the perspective of a boy and a girl. In its own little way, *To Kill a Mockingbird* nudged Americans into hastening the end of Jim Crow.

THOUGHT FOR TODAY: The court of public opinion is an important one when making social change. Novels bring characters from all backgrounds into the minds and hearts of readers...and often change the world for the better.

JULY 12: MALALA STANDS UP FOR EDUCATION

I do not even hate the Talib who shot me. Even if there is a gun in my hand and he stands in front of me. I would not shoot him.

~ Malala Yousafzai ~

Malala Yousafzai was blogging about girls' education in Pakistan for the BBC when Taliban assassins shot her. She nearly died but recovered after treatment in England. She would go on to win the Nobel Peace prize for her advocacy of education for girls.

Until recent years there was a wide education gap between boys and girls. Now, even in less developed countries, elementary education is the new normal for both boys and girls alike. As nearly all children around the world attend school, literacy rates have jumped substantially.

THOUGHT FOR TODAY: In 1970 less than half of adults in developing countries could read. Today the global youth literacy rate is 91%, which is higher than the literacy rates in rich countries just one or two generations ago. We live in an age of unprecedented education access and literacy.

JULY 13: ARTIFICIAL INTELLIGENCE

The iPhone is made on a global scale, and it blends computers, the Internet, communications, and artificial intelligence in one blockbuster innovation.

~ Tyler Cowen ~

In the 1950s, at the dawn of the Computer Age, a group of academics met at Dartmouth College to discuss the nature and possibilities of "thinking machines." The Dartmouth Workshop, as it would be called, was the brainchild of professor John McCarthy. In July 1956 he brought together some of the best minds in computers. McCarthy used the expression "artificial intelligence" (AI) because it was the most inclusive term that he could think of for the diverse group of scholars he assembled. The gathering was essentially a loose series of brainstorming sessions that became a seminal touchstone in the history of computing.

 **THOUGHT FOR TODAY:** AI is an important part of 21st century life, even if we do not see it directly. It helps doctors diagnose disease, students learn math, and computers fix their own bugs.

JULY 14: COMPETITION AND COOPERATION

But does that mean that war and violence are inevitable?
I would argue not because we have also evolved this
amazingly sophisticated intellect.

~ Jane Goodall ~

On this day in 1960, Jane Goodall entered the Gombe Reserve in Tanzania to study its chimpanzees. Goodall had no formal training, but she was a quick study and found ways to observe the chimps up close. She spent thousands of hours taking notes and discovered they had unique personalities and used tools. Goodall found that chimps were similar to humans in many ways, including affection, intelligence and relationships. Goodall also saw violence amongst chimps. Until that time, many scientists thought other primates were noble savages, but like humans, chimps have their dark and bright sides.

THOUGHT FOR TODAY: Tennyson's phrase that nature is "red in tooth and claw" may be true, but the more we study our cousins—great apes like chimps, bonobos and orangutans—the more we see that cooperation is also baked into our primate genes.

JULY 15: THE SPACE RACE RUNS TOGETHER

You develop an instant global consciousness, an intense dissatisfaction with the state of the world, and a compulsion to do something about it.

~ Edgar Mitchell, on seeing earth from space ~

The US was thunderstruck when the USSR successfully launched *Sputnik* in 1957. Americans feared Russian nukes falling from space, and US schools revamped math and science programs. The United States would catch up and surpass the Soviet space program when NASA sent men to the moon in 1969.

The warring powers would come together in space as Cold War tensions warmed. On this day in 1975, American and Soviet rockets launched astronauts into space, and Apollo and Soyuz spacecraft would dock in space two days later. It was a symbolic end of the space race.

THOUGHT FOR TODAY: The Apollo-Soyuz mission was a bellwether for US-Russian cooperation in space and the coming end to the Cold War. Today the US and Russia work closely together on several important space projects.

JULY 16: IDA B. WELLS: RISKING ALL TO FIGHT JIM CROW

One had better die fighting against injustice than to die like a dog or a rat in a trap.

~ Ida B. Wells ~

It took incredible courage for black civil rights activists to stand up to the racist forces that ruled America. Ida B. Wells was one of the heroes that risked life and limb for righteousness' sake.

Wells was born on this day in 1862 to enslaved parents who became active in the Republican Party. In her early 20s she refused to move from the first-class carriage of her train, an act that crystallized her purpose in life. Wells became a journalist and wrote about the injustices of racism, especially lynchings.

THOUGHT FOR TODAY: Ida B. Wells risked her life to bring to light the brutality of lynchings in America. Her activism brought widespread attention to lynching, and she was one of the founders of the NAACP.

JULY 17: AHHHHH, AC!

Owners of valuable works of art don't give to institutions that don't provide good air conditioning.

~ Stanley Marcus ~

On this day in 1902, Willis Carrier designed the first modern air-conditioning system. Air conditioning is now a standard feature in most homes and businesses in wealthy countries and, increasingly, around the world. In the United States, the spread of air conditioning facilitated the Sun Belt boom in the late 20th century. AC also led to greater productivity in the summer months. Air conditioning saves lives, especially the young and elderly, during heat waves. And it feels good on a hot day.

THOUGHT FOR TODAY: Air conditioning is both a luxury and a necessity. It is a luxury in that humans lived without it until very recently. Nonetheless, the many benefits of AC should not be underestimated, including saved lives during heat waves, increased productivity, and comfort. Air conditioning also maintains optimal humidity and filters the air.

JULY 18: INTEL FOUNDED

Failures are not something to be avoided. You want to have them happen as quickly as you can so you can make progress rapidly.

~ Gordon Moore ~

One hallmark of human progress is miniaturization. This is the process by which each succeeding generation of inventions tends to be smaller and thus more efficient. Miniaturization has had its biggest impact in electronics. Once we used vacuum tubes for electronic devices, but then the transistor was invented, and after that the integrated microchip.

On this day in 1968, microchip pioneers Robert Noyce and Gordon Moore founded Intel. This company created microchips for many of the computers that powered the Information Age. Intel is still big in its field, although Samsung has surpassed it in terms of revenue.

THOUGHT FOR TODAY: Gordon Moore's Law, the insight that the number of transistors in an integrated circuit doubles about every two years, has proved true. This computing power brings information, communication and tools to everyone at ever-decreasing prices.

JULY 19: BETTER CARE FOR CHILDREN

For just a few dollars a dose, vaccines save lives and help reduce poverty. They are safe and effective. They ensure healthier children, families and communities.

~ Seth Berkley ~

In early times, the health of children was considered the provenance of the mother. Few specialized services were offered by governments. In the 19th century, middle-class women and doctors were publicizing their concerns about children's health, especially among the industrial poor.

One response to this concern was the growth of children's hospitals, the first of which was the Necker-Enfants Malades Hospital in Paris (1802), followed a half century later by the Great Ormond Street Hospital in London (1852). On this day in 1869, Boston Children's Hospital was founded by Francis Henry Brown, a Civil War surgeon.

 **THOUGHT FOR TODAY:** The growth of children's hospitals pushed down child mortality rates and improved children's health and medical care. Hundreds of children's hospitals exist around the world, thanks in part to the medical pioneers in the 1800s.

JULY 20: MAN ON THE MOON

That's one small step for man, one giant leap for mankind.

~ Neil Armstrong ~

On this day in 1969, NASA fulfilled John F. Kennedy's promise of putting men on the moon before the end of the decade. Apollo 11 astronauts Neil Armstrong and Buzz Aldrin walked on the moon, planted a flag, and gathered moon rocks. A trip to the moon was the stuff of science fiction until NASA made it happen.

Space exploration continues today. Since the Apollo program, many countries have launched satellites that have explored the planets and moons in the solar system. Humans now have a constant presence in space on the International Space Station, and plans are underway to send astronauts to Mars.

THOUGHT FOR TODAY: Humanity's ability to innovate and explore seems almost endless. Space exploration has expanded scientific understanding and human imagination and shows no signs of stopping.

JULY 21: THE NATO TREATY IS RATIFIED

Truman is seen as a near-great president because he put in place the containment doctrine boosted by the Truman Doctrine, the Marshall Plan and NATO.

~ Robert Dallek ~

Historically, alliances have been formed in anticipation of future conquests. The North Atlantic Treaty Organization (NATO) was founded to prevent them. On this day in 1949, the United States Senate ratified the NATO treaty that created the alliance that was a bulwark against Communist Russia and its Eastern Europe allies. Ironically, NATO never engaged in military operations until after the end of the Cold War.

THOUGHT FOR TODAY: Today there are few interstate wars. NATO and other security arrangements have made war an unpopular and ever-more-infrequent choice for states hoping to forward national aims through violence. As Steven Pinker demonstrated in his book The Better Angels of Our Nature, war and violence are near all-time lows.

JULY 22: THE NEW COLOSSUS

Give me your tired, your poor,

Your huddled masses yearning to breathe free

~ Emma Lazarus ~

Approximately 65,000 years ago, humans migrated out of Africa and colonized the rest of the world. In modern times, migration has been sped by ships, trains and airplanes. Many countries like the United States, Canada and Argentina, are peopled by overseas immigrants. The identity of these countries has been formed by the immigrants from Africa, Europe, Asia and other regions.

Today is the birthday of Emma Lazarus, who wrote the poem "The New Colossus," which was inscribed on a bronze plaque on the pedestal of the Statue of Liberty in New York Harbor.

THOUGHT FOR TODAY: The diversity of immigrants in countries like the US has made these places rich mixes of culture, ideas, energies and histories. For many years, immigrants were encouraged to assimilate. Today we embrace diversity knowing it makes us all—and the world—better.

JULY 23: THE FATHER OF GENETICS

My scientific studies have afforded me great gratification; and I am convinced that it will not be long before the whole world acknowledges the results of my work.

~ Gregor Mendel ~

Gregor Mendel was a Czech monk who experimented in obscurity with his pea plants. Through much observation, data recording, and deep thought, Mendel determined the basic laws of genetics. It took several decades before his ideas were discovered at the turn of the 20th century, at which point the field of genetics was launched.

On this day in 2016, The Mendel Museum in Brno, Czech Republic, opened the exhibition *Gregor Johann Mendel - The Story of a Humble Genius.*

THOUGHT FOR TODAY: Genetics has come a long way since Mendel founded the field in the 1800s, but without his first steps, we would not have come this far. Today people can find a detailed history of their origins through genetic testing, and doctors can screen patients for genetic diseases.

JULY 24: PROGRESS IN MENTAL HEALTH

There are three musts that hold us back: I must do well. You must treat me well. And the world must be easy.

~ Albert Ellis ~

On this day in 2007, Albert Ellis, one of the great psychotherapists of the 20th century, died. When Ellis earned his Ph.D. in the late 1940s, he, like most psychologists, believed that Freud's psychoanalysis was the best treatment for patients suffering from mental illness. As he studied psychoanalysis more deeply, his faith waned. By 1953 he developed Rational Therapy, which was a very directive approach (in contrast to the free association methods of psychoanalysis). For many years Ellis was dismissed by his colleagues, but by the 1970s, Ellis was seen as one of the leading lights in psychotherapeutic practice.

THOUGHT FOR TODAY: Albert Ellis was a psychotherapy pioneer that moved psychology away from Freud's darkly sexual (and unproven) models of the psyche toward Ellis' rational cognitive approach where patients take charge of their thinking and mental health.

JULY 25: TEST TUBE BABIES

The management of fertility is one of the most important functions of adulthood.

~ *Germaine Greer* ~

We often forget that childbirth is a dangerous thing. Our large brains are an unrivaled advantage for survival. We are problem-solving Swiss Army knives because of the flexibility of our learning and thinking. Our large heads mean that childbirth is painful and dangerous. "Died in childbirth" was a common cause of death for young women, but maternal mortality has dropped remarkably in the last century.

Infertility has also bedeviled families. Add our modern trend of having babies later, and infertility challenges are magnified. On this day in 1978, Louise Joy Brown was born, the first human conceived by in vitro fertilization (IVF). Since then, approximately five million babies have been born from IVF procedures.

THOUGHT FOR TODAY: Infertility was once considered an unsolvable puzzle. Today IVF and other procedures can give mothers and their families new opportunities to become parents.

JULY 26: HUMAN RIGHTS EXPAND FOR THE DISABLED

The ADA is the living testament to our nation's commitment that we will always stand up for our neighbors' right to live fulfilling lives.

~ Tammy Duckworth ~

Several American presidents lived with disabilities, but the most famous was Franklin Roosevelt. Nonetheless, his difficulty walking because of polio was mostly hidden. Members of the press were encouraged not to photograph him in his wheelchair. This hiding of disabilities was commonplace. Those who lived with disabilities had to fend for themselves without much public help.

A milestone in the quest for equal rights for the disabled happened on this day in 1990 when George H.W. Bush signed the Americans with Disabilities Act (ADA) into law. It mandated equal opportunities for people of all abilities.

THOUGHT FOR TODAY: One of many positive threads in human history is the provision of rights and services for people of all kinds. The ADA recognized the needs of millions of Americans who had previously been victims of discrimination.

JULY 27: THE GENEVA CONVENTIONS

I believe the United States must remain a standard bearer in the conduct of war. We lose ourselves when we compromise the very ideals that we fight to defend.

~ Barack Obama ~

All's fair in love and war. This truism has characterized military conflict for most of history. In 1864, the first Geneva Convention established guidelines for the Red Cross and other relief forces, as well as rules of war for more humane treatment.

On this day in 1929, the Convention Relative to the Treatment of Prisoners of War was signed by representatives of 53 countries. It prohibited reprisals and collective penalties and set guidelines for the prisoners of war.

 **THOUGHT FOR TODAY:** The several Geneva Conventions created rules of war and treatment of prisoners. While combatants don't always abide by the rules of war, the Geneva Conventions are well known guidelines that states are pressured to follow.

JULY 28: TERRORISM FAILS...AGAIN

The overwhelming majority of people in Ireland and Northern Ireland voted in favour of the agreement signed on Good Friday 1998.

~ Queen Elizabeth II ~

The Troubles were Northern Ireland's 30-year civil war between Unionists (primarily Protestant) and Republicans (primarily Catholic) that brought misery to the country. The Troubles were a cycle of conflict and violence in which protests begat military response that often turned violent. This cycle meant that Northern Ireland, like the Middle East, became synonymous with endless conflict.

But the conflict ended. On this day in 2005 the Provisional IRA said it would end its participation in the Northern Ireland conflict. Within a few months, officials confirmed that the Provisional IRA had been totally disarmed.

THOUGHT FOR TODAY: Terrorism—by both Republican and Unionist forces—exhausted and alienated the people of Northern Ireland and the international community. Terrorism failed and the peaceful process initiated by the Good Friday Agreement of 1998 is mending the wounds caused by the Troubles.

JULY 29: THE SCOUTING MOVEMENT MARCHES

The Girl Scouts is where I became acquainted with the idea that a woman can do anything.

~ Lisa Ling ~

British army officer Robert Baden-Powell was concerned that army recruits lacked initiative, decision making, and leadership skills. While serving in the Second Boer War, he wrote *Aids to Scouting* with an aim to improve these skills. On this day in 1907, Robert Baden-Powell set up the first scout camp on Brownsea Island Scout camp in Poole Harbour, England. Three days later he opened the first camp, which still operates scouting events to this day. In the years that followed, the Scouting movement, for both boys and girls, would form spontaneously, inspired by Baden-Powell and other pioneers.

THOUGHT FOR TODAY: The scouting movement would go on to help millions of children learn many skills not taught in schools. Because of its engaging hands-on, experiential, and expeditionary learning components, Scouting gave young people experience they both enjoyed and benefited from.

JULY 30: CARE FOR ELDERS, AID FOR THE POOR

The 40-hour work week, the minimum wage, health insurance, Social Security, Medicare. The cornerstones of middle-class security all bear the union label.

~ Barack Obama ~

Three score and ten years was reckoned by Biblical authors to be the length of a human life. This was a bit optimistic. It did not account for high mortality rates for children and the death of mothers in childbirth, let alone plague, famine and war.

In recent decades, as more food and better medicine have lengthened lifespans, governments have created programs to buffer the lives of the poor and elderly. On this day in 1965, President Lyndon Johnson signed the Social Security Amendments that created Medicare and Medicaid.

THOUGHT FOR TODAY: Some are calling seventy "the new fifty" as our elders are living longer, better lives with improved nutrition and healthcare. Nowadays life expectancy is in the low 80s in some countries, meaning much of the population will live into the 90s and beyond.

JULY 31: FROM SAILS TO STEAM TO SCREW PROPELLERS

Set your course by the stars, not by the lights of every passing ship.

~ Omar Bradley ~

The 19th century was a time of revolutionary improvements in nautical technology. In 1800, sails propelled boats across the water, but by 1900, the *SS America*, with coal-fired boilers driving a single screw propeller, could travel 22 miles per hour. One of the great innovators of the 1800s was John Ericsson, who was born this day in 1803. He created a hot air engine, designed and built the first ironclad fighting ship, improved torpedoes, and played an important role in developing screw propellers.

THOUGHT FOR TODAY: With improvements in ship technology, the world was brought closer together. Migration from Europe to the Americas—and travel throughout the world—accelerated quickly during the 1800s. Today most people fly when they travel to faraway destinations, and most passengers on seagoing ships are there for a vacation.

AUGUST 1: CONCERT FOR BANGLADESH

Bangladesh is a world of metaphor, of high and low theater, of great poetry and music. You talk to a rice farmer and you find a poet.

~ Jean Houston ~

East Pakistan, which became Bangladesh in 1971, went through horrific struggles when it split from West Pakistan. War and a tropical cyclone killed hundreds of thousands and displaced millions. Former Beatle George Harrison organized concerts to raise awareness and funds for struggling Bangladesh. The concerts were successful and became a template for future fundraising efforts, notably Live Aid.

Today Bangladesh is a country transformed. Birth rates and death rates have decreased while income and education have improved dramatically. Bangladesh is a fast-growing country that is integrated into the world economy.

 **THOUGHT FOR TODAY:** Decolonization and the many wars in its aftermath wrecked much destruction and suffering on the world. Bangladesh's split with West Pakistan was one such episode. However, westerners showed compassion and made efforts to help. Most importantly, Bangladesh reformed and became more democratic.

AUGUST 2: FIRST CENSUS TAKEN

The goal is to turn data into information, and information into insight.

~ Carly Fiorina ~

The US Constitution dictates that a census of the populace be taken every ten years to determine taxation and representation in Congress. This data gathering helps the government craft better programs. Since the first census, government data gathering has increased significantly so that agencies can diagnose problems and find solutions for social, economic and educational challenges. Nowadays, data gathering pervades nearly every profession, and powerful computer computers crunch very large data sets. We live in an era of big data where complex systems like weather patterns can be understood in much greater depth, which means that our predictions are much better.

 **THOUGHT FOR TODAY:** Data collection is a basic building block of a science, and by collecting and analyzing data of all kinds, we have a better understanding of our world.

AUGUST 3: RUBBER CHANGES THE WORLD

The condom has saved so many lives, and it'll save so many more lives. We really owe a great deal to the rubber tree.

~ Mechai Viravaidya ~

Sealing in—and out—liquids has been a challenge for thousands of years. When inventors learned how to vulcanize rubber, which made it both easier to mold and more durable, rubber was used for erasers, rain jackets, and seals. Rubber also revolutionized electricity insulation and, later, transportation when companies manufactured inflatable tires for bicycles and automobiles.

On this day in 1900, the Firestone Tire and Rubber Company was founded. Like other rubber companies, Firestone manufactures tires and other rubber products that help us grip the road, seal things tight, insulate electricity, and keep out water.

 **THOUGHT FOR TODAY:** Rubber is one of hundreds of everyday, easy-to-overlook inventions that have made life much safer and more comfortable. It seals, grips and bends. May we never forget all the tiny wonders that make our lives better!

AUGUST 4: THE BIRTH OF BUBBLY

Remember, gentlemen, it's not just France we are fighting for, it's champagne!

*~ **Winston Churchill** ~*

Come quickly, I am tasting the stars! is what Dom Perignon supposedly said when he invented champagne...only he almost certainly did not invent champagne. Nonetheless, August 4, 1693 is celebrated as the day Perignon birthed bubbly.

The guidelines that vintners are required to follow to make champagne constitute the longest rulebook of any wine in the world. Because of the powerful gas buildup from refermentation, thicker glass was needed for the bottles, as was the use of special corks. Most champagne drinkers agree that all the special attention afforded the cultivation and creation of this special wine are worth it. Today victories, special occasions, and new years are greeted with champagne toasts.

 **THOUGHT FOR TODAY:** Champagne—like chocolate, coffee, good sex, and true love—is one of many precious delights that make life wonderful.

AUGUST 5: FLOGGINGS WILL NOT CONTINUE

Power based on love is a thousand times more effective and permanent then the one derived from fear of punishment.

~ Mahatma Gandhi ~

Beatings and spankings have been a part of "discipline" for a long time. Only in the past few hundred years have more compassionate approaches eclipsed old brutal ways. The Royal Navy was famed for its intricate set of flogging procedures and customs, including "flogging around the fleet." This punishment entailed a convicted sailor getting flogged, up to 600 times, on different ships. On this day in 1861, the US Army abolished flogging as a disciplinary measure for its soldiers. The Royal Navy finally did so in 1881.

THOUGHT FOR TODAY: If corporal punishment worked then crimes should be going up now that we eschew these brutal methods. On the contrary, as the criminal justice system has become less brutal, crime has gone down. Many scholars argue that the 21st century is the most peaceful era in history.

AUGUST 6: WWW

The Web as I envisaged it, we have not seen it yet. The future is still so much bigger than the past.

~ Tim Berners-Lee ~

The history of advances in communications could serve as a good proxy for human progress. At some point our paleolithic ancestors developed language and art. In the last 5000 years, writing developed in several places around the world. The printing press made the dissemination of knowledge easier, and literacy proliferated as a result.

The advent of the internet and the World Wide Web has been another quantum leap. On this day in 1991, Tim Berners-Lee published a description of the Web that can still be viewed at http://info.cern.ch/hypertext/WWW/TheProject.html.

THOUGHT FOR TODAY: Advances in communication mean that billions of people have instant access to the sum total of human knowledge. Approximately 75% of humanity is now literate, rates unthinkably high even 50 years ago. The internet means access to information and education has never been easier.

AUGUST 7: THE CAR, FREEDOM AND FEMINISM

Remember, Ginger Rogers did everything Fred Astaire did, but backwards and in high heels.

~ Faith Whittlesey ~

Patriarchal societies have been controlling women for too long. In some corners of the world, women are still confined indoors and must be accompanied by men when leaving the home. Women's rights expanded in the 1800s thanks to the efforts of suffragists and civil rights advocates. In the 20th century, the automobile also expanded horizons for women. Cars offered mobility and an escape from prying eyes of local busybodies.

On this day in 1909, four women completed a cross-country drive from New York to San Francisco, a first for women. Their independence was shocking a hundred years ago, but such a trip is commonplace today.

THOUGHT FOR TODAY: The history of women's freedom and rights have been one of progress. While change has often happened at too slow a pace, the change has been overwhelmingly positive.

AUGUST 8: 8888 UPRISING IN BURMA

If you look at the democratic process as a game of chess, there have to be many, many moves before you get to checkmate.

~ Aung San Suu Kyi ~

Until the 1930s there were no democracies in South and Southeast Asia. Today most countries in the region are democracies or moving from autocracy toward democracy. Burma (Myanmar) is one of these nations. On this day in 1988, thousands of demonstrators took the streets and protested the military government. While the government crushed these protests, many of the 8888 demonstrators went on to lead the Saffron Revolution in 2007.

Until 2011, Burma was a hermit country ruled by a military autocracy. Nobel Peace Prize laureate Aung San Suu Kyi and others led the push for democratic reforms, and she was elected State Counsellor in 2015.

THOUGHT FOR TODAY: The transition from autocracy to democracy is rarely a smooth one. Nonetheless, the broad if bumpy trend toward democracy continues in the 21st century.

AUGUST 9: ANESTHESIA

A doctor in a hospital told me that when the mujaheddin were fighting in the early 90s, he often performed amputations and Caesarean sections without anesthesia.

~ Khaled Hosseini ~

Imagine surgery without anesthesia. A harrowing moment in *Gone with the Wind* features an amputation performed on a man who screams and wails through the procedure. Of course, since there were no antibiotics during the Civil War, survival after such procedures was touch and go.

On this day on 1819, dental surgeon and anesthesia pioneer William Morton was born in Massachusetts. In 1846 he gave the first successful public demonstration of ether anesthesia during surgery. This success was publicized and led to a general acceptance of the use of anesthesia.

THOUGHT FOR TODAY: Today millions of people are given general anesthesia in procedures both simple and complex. As science has progressed, so too has anesthesia, which today is safer and has fewer side effects.

AUGUST 10: CONSTRUCTION STARTS IN GREENWICH

It is clear to everyone that astronomy compels the soul to look upward and draws it from the things of this world to the other.

~ Plato ~

On this day in 1675, the first stones were laid in the building of the Royal Observatory, Greenwich. This observatory would come to play a crucial role in the history of navigation and astronomy. It famously became the location through which the Prime Meridien passed between the North and South poles, as well as the place from which Greenwich Mean Time was determined.

Breakthroughs in science can answer cosmic questions or solve practical problems. The Royal Observatory, Greenwich, played a role in both of these pursuits and led to work that knitted the world more closely together.

 **THOUGHT FOR TODAY:** When you look at the time on your smart phone or watch, recall that time-keeping was imprecise for most of history. Today we have an infrastructure for precise timekeeping that allows us to keep track of and use time efficiently.

AUGUST 11: A FAMILY'S STORY TRANSFIXES AMERICA

My fondest hope is that Roots may start black, white, brown, red, yellow people digging back for their own roots.

~ Alex Haley ~

Genealogy research is a popular passion in the United States. This passion became a craze when Alex Haley, who was born on this day in 1921, wrote a book about his family, *Roots*. It became a bestseller and the most popular TV show of its time. The *Roots* phenomenon was all the more extraordinary given it was a history of an African-American family—from Africa, through slavery, to Jim Crow, and then modern times. The popular series set TV viewing records and presented African Americans front and center on evening television. Up to that time, TV featured few primetime dramas about black Americans.

THOUGHT FOR TODAY: The stories of all Americans are finally being told. National media formerly featured whites in traditional roles. Roots was another national event that changed American culture and conversation for the better.

AUGUST 12: ANTISEPTIC SURGERY

I am utterly convinced that Science and Peace will triumph over Ignorance and War, that nations will eventually unite not to destroy but to edify.

~ Louis Pasteur ~

In the early 1800s, surgeons wore surgery stains like badges of honor. Between operations, they neither changed clothes nor washed hands. Despite the germ theory insights of Ignaz Semmelweis, surgeons operated in unsanitary conditions.

But on this date in 1865, Joseph Lister conducted the first surgery in antiseptic conditions. He used carbolic acid to clean surgical theaters and instruments, and Lister directed all medical staff to clean their hands before and after surgery with a five percent carbolic acid solution. Infections decreased and Lister's ideas spread. A century after his first antiseptic surgery, he was deemed the "Father of Modern Surgery."

 **THOUGHT FOR TODAY:** Many of the most important medical breakthroughs have been forgotten. Today's doctors are standing on the shoulders of giants like Joseph Lister, who made surgery much safer for patients going under the knife.

AUGUST 13: NATIONAL SAFETY COUNCIL INCORPORATED BY CONGRESS

Carefulness costs you nothing. Carelessness may cost you your life.

~ Anonymous ~

In the 19th century, the American workplace was "unusually dangerous" according to scholar Mark Aldrich at Smith College. Accidents were considered cheap, a small price to pay in dangerous industries like mining and the railroads. But workers demanding better conditions during the Progressive Era, and government regulation led to much safer workplaces. Workers compensation schemes proliferated in the 20th century, which spurred employers to improve working conditions. Another safety landmark was the creation of the National Safety Council by Congress, which was incorporated on this day in 1953.

THOUGHT FOR TODAY: A marker of human progress has been the increasing value of human life. The National Safety Council has been one of many organizations that have made life much safer than it has ever been.

AUGUST 14: SOCIAL SECURITY PROTECTS OLDER AMERICANS

People who are hungry and out of a job are the stuff of which dictatorships are made.

~ Franklin D. Roosevelt ~

Historically, elderly people have relied on relatives and savings to ensure survival once they could no longer work. In the 1800s, German Chancellor Otto von Bismarck initiated the first large-scale national retirement insurance. Other countries followed suit. America did not adopt its own form of national retirement insurance until Franklin Roosevelt signed the Social Security Act on this day in 1935.

THOUGHT FOR TODAY: Social Security made the lives of the elderly safer and more stable. The guaranteed income also stimulated the economy as this income is almost always spent on necessities. The 20th century brought greater prosperity, education, and technological advancement, and with these achievements, governments have also ensured stability and safety for older Americans.

AUGUST 15: THE PANAMA CANAL OPENS TO TRAFFIC

A finer body of men has never been gathered by any nation than the men who have done the work of building the Panama Canal

~ Theodore Roosevelt ~

To travel between the Atlantic and Pacific Oceans, it once was necessary to "round the Horn"—Cape Horn. Passage around the Cape is dangerous because of high winds, stormy seas, and icebergs. On top of that, Cape Horn is nearly 56 degrees south latitude, far from Europe and East Asia, two of the most important nodes of world trade.

To shorten the trip around the Horn, the US built the Panama Canal, which opened this day in 1914. The Canal is still in use 100 years later and working at full capacity. The Panamanian government widened and deepened the Canal to accommodate larger modern ships.

THOUGHT FOR TODAY: World travel and trade have spread people, ideas and commerce to all corners of the world. The Panama Canal is an achievement in itself and significantly eases world trade.

AUGUST 16: THE MIGRATORY BIRD TREATY

Bird migration is the one truly unifying natural phenomenon in the world, stitching the continents together.

~ Scott Weidensaul ~

Until recent centuries, there were few legal restrictions on hunting. Though customs curtailed indiscriminate hunting, many animals were shot and trapped into extinction. Concern for bird species increased in the late 1800s as feathers became fashionable in ladies' hats, a trend that decimated bird populations. Local chapters of the Audubon Society, named in honor of naturalist John James Audubon, organized feather boycotts and lobbied for a treaty to protect migratory birds.

The work of the Audubon Society and the growing environmental movement of the early 20th century helped craft the Migratory Bird Treaty, which was signed this day in 1916.

THOUGHT FOR TODAY: In the last hundred years, we have worked hard to preserve nature and the animal world. The Migratory Bird Treaty is a cornerstone of the wildlife conservation movement that is so important in life today.

AUGUST 17: BIRTHS, MARRIAGES, DEATHS

Basic science is a building block for scientific innovation and economic growth in the information age.

~ Tim Bishop ~

Data can seem pretty dull, but in truth it's very important. Gather accurate vital statistics of a population and you can determine the most common causes of illness and death and then craft policies to make people live healthier, happier lives. On this day in 1836, the British Parliament approved the registration of births, deaths and marriages.

Governmental information gathering has led to public health breakthroughs, and data collection helps legislatures draft laws that reflect the real needs of their constituents.

THOUGHT FOR TODAY: We live in the Information Age. In the last few centuries, as data collection has increased, so too has our ability to respond to problems and opportunities that data bring to light. Data collection has helped improve government, public health, business, education and other fields.

AUGUST 18: JAMES MEREDITH GRADUATES FROM OLE MISS

My objective was to force the federal government into a position where they would have to use military force to enforce my rights as a citizen.

~ James Meredith ~

After the Enlightenment, and especially in the 1800s, reformers agitated for primary education for children. By 1900, most states in the US had compulsory schooling laws. Despite these gains, racist segregation laws meant that white schools were given better resources than black schools.

On this day in 1963, James Meredith graduated from the University of Mississippi. He was the first African American to do so. After rejections by Ole Miss, he used the courts to overturn the rejections. He entered the university to choruses of racist epithets and was shot several times. Meredith recovered and prevailed.

THOUGHT FOR TODAY: Until recent decades, black Americans were systematically excluded from most universities in America. Today they make up approximately 15% of college enrollment. Pioneers like James Meredith broke down barriers and made America better.

AUGUST 19: FROM RICHARD TO RENÉE

(I wanted) to prove that transsexuals as well as other persons fighting social stigmas can hold their heads up high.

~ Renée Richards ~

You're either a man or a woman. Such was the social norm until the late 20th century, but one woman took a stand and changed the world.

Richard Raskin, who was born this day in 1934, had sex reassignment surgery and changed her name to Renée Richards. She then moved to Newport Beach, California where her strong tennis game drew attention and publicity, but the United States Tennis Association (USTA) made it clear she would not be able to play as a women. Not prone to taking stands and fighting fights, Richards nonetheless sued the USTA and won.

THOUGHT FOR TODAY: Richards was a trailblazer like James Meredith and Rosa Parks. Her successes paved the way for the millions of LGBT people who followed her to gain the acceptance and respect they deserved.

AUGUST 20: YELLOWSTONE BURNS HOTTEST

It is known that wildfires behave unpredictably but it is my experience that humans in the presence of wildfire are also likely to behave in unpredictable ways.

~ Michael Leunig ~

For nearly 100 years, fire suppression was the policy of the US Forest Service. This prevented thousands of fires but hastened the build-up of forest fuel. By the late 1980s, the Forest Service had begun a prescribed burn program to burn off excessive fuel loads, but that did not prevent the catastrophic Yellowstone fires of 1988.

August 20, 1988 was termed "Black Saturday" for the thick smoke and intense fires of that day. Autumn brought moisture and cooler temperatures, and eventually all the fires burned out. Approximately one-third of Yellowstone had burned.

THOUGHT FOR TODAY: Many scientists and nature lovers feared the 1988 fires would scar Yellowstone forever. Scientists now think that intense fire seasons periodically happen and are part of the rhythm of the Yellowstone ecosystem. Today the Yellowstone forests are growing back.

AUGUST 21: FROM DISASTER, HEALING

My own religion has been to do all the good I could to my fellow men, and as little harm as possible.

~ W. W. Mayo ~

On this day in 1883, an F5 tornado struck Rochester, Minnesota. Rochester resident William Worrall Mayo established a temporary hospital for the injured survivors. Aided by Mother Mary Alfred Moes and the Sisters of Saint Francis, Moes asked Mayo if he would collaborate to create a hospital in Rochester. From these humble roots the world-famous Mayo Clinic was founded.

Today some 4700 doctors and scientists are supported by more than 55,000 healthcare staff. The Clinic is noted for medical breakthroughs, including the discovery and use of cortisone.

THOUGHT FOR TODAY: According to the UN, world average life expectancy in 2010-2015 was more than 71 years. In 1880 life expectancy was less than half that. The work of hundreds of medical research institutions, like the Mayo Clinic, have improved the quality and increased the length of life.

AUGUST 22: ELECTRON MICROSCOPY

How little do we discover in comparison of those things which now are and forever will be hidden from our sight?

~ Anton van Leeuwenhoek ~

When Anton van Leeuwenhoek made the first practical microscope in the 1600s, he was able to magnify objects up to 270 times. Today, the best light microscopes can magnify objects more than 2000 times.

But microscopy was truly revolutionized when scientists created electron microscopes in the 1920s. James Hillier, who was born this day in 1915, was part of the team who invented the first electron microscope in North America. The electron microscope meant that scientists could examine basic plant and animal cell structures, viruses, and even molecules and atoms.

THOUGHT FOR TODAY: Our ability to see the smallest building blocks of matter and life mean we can understand them more deeply. The electron microscope is one of the many tools that were the stuff of science fiction...until they were created through human ingenuity and hard work.

AUGUST 23: CHURCHES UNITED FOR PEACE

God's dream is that you and I and all of us will realize that we are family

~ Desmond Tutu ~

One subplot of world religious history is sectarianism. Religions are founded by a prophet and soon after his death, the successors squabble over doctrine and governance. Since its founding, Christianity has broken into hundreds of sects. However, on this day in 1948, delegates from 147 church organizations met to create the World Council of Churches (WCC). Besides working together to proselytize, the WCC has been an active proponent of peace journalism. The WCC supports peace journalism in order to highlight the good works done by Christians and non-Christians alike who make the world safer, more civil, and more peaceful.

THOUGHT FOR TODAY: In the past, religious organizations often supported aggressive war to spread the faith. Today many religious organizations are united in their opposition to war and actively work for peaceful solutions to local, national and international conflicts.

AUGUST 24: WILBERFORCE: A FORCE FOR REFORM

God Almighty has set before me two great objects, the suppression of the Slave Trade and the Reformation of Manners (morals).

~ William Wilberforce ~

A deep faith in God and human goodness drives many to dedicate themselves to making the world better. William Wilberforce, who was born on this day in 1759, had a religious reawakening that caused him to change his life and purpose. In the late 1780s, Wilberforce was convinced to join the slave trade abolition movement.

What ensued was the first grassroots civil rights campaign that involved people from all classes. While the campaign was not finally successful until the passing of the Slave Trade Act in 1807, it was an important victory against a horrid institution.

THOUGHT FOR TODAY: Whether driven by spiritual, moral or personal motives, social reformers apply their zeal to win rights for more and more people. Today reformers work to end child marriage, ensure education for all, and guarantee equal rights for LGBT citizens.

AUGUST 25: PETER SHEPHERD, FIRST AID PIONEER

Safety brings first aid to the uninjured

~ F.S. Hughes ~

Nowadays, nearly everyone is taught some first aid, such as CPR and the Heimlich Maneuver. But for most of history, these methods were not known, used or taught. It took British Army doctor Peter Shepherd, who was born on this day in 1841, to invent first aid. He, along with Colonel Francis Duncan, established first aid training in the British Army and later applied what they learned to teaching civilians. Now first aid skills are taught around the world to hundreds of millions of people.

 **THOUGHT FOR TODAY:** One reason that rates of deaths and injury from accidents is at an all-time low is because everyday citizens know how to respond to accidents. Today millions of lives are saved because of the trained responses of everyday people to events that used to kill and maim.

AUGUST 26: THANK GOD FOR TOILET PAPER!

Rules governing defecation, hygiene and pollution exist in every culture at every period in history. It may in fact be the foundation of civilization

~ Rose George ~

August 26 is National Toilet Paper Day in the United States, for on this day in 1871 the first roll of toilet paper was sold. Before TP, people used pebbles, corn cobs, leaves, ferns, moss, hay, fruit skins, seashells...anything at hand. In more recent times cheap printed items like the Sears Roebuck catalogue served for post defecation wiping. With modern flush toilets, degradable toilet paper was necessary lest sewage lines get blocked.

THOUGHT FOR TODAY: We should not for a minute take the flush toilet, toilet paper, and hand washing for granted, though the ubiquity of sanitary defecation makes it easy to forget. One of the UN's Sustainable Development Goals is to end open defecation, a once unthinkable goal that now is within our grasp—or flush—to achieve.

AUGUST 27: A PROCESS THAT YIELDS MORE FOOD

If you desire peace, cultivate justice, but at the same time cultivate the fields to produce more bread; otherwise there will be no peace.

~ Norman Borlaug ~

Soil nutrient depletion is the bane of every farmer. Over time, fields lose important nutrients and yields decrease. Humans are ingenious, and our farming forebears found ways to increase yields, through slash-and-burn techniques, manure fertilizer, and even mining bird guano from islands. But all these sources get depleted.

In 1905, German chemist Fritz Haber discovered how to fix atmospheric nitrogen to make ammonia for fertilizer. His associate Carl Bosch—born on this day in 1874—pioneered large scale methods for fixing nitrogen.

THOUGHT FOR TODAY: The Haber-Bosch process of creating fertilizer has significantly increased agricultural yields. Despite that fact that world population is above seven billion, we have never had this much food, and starvation and malnutrition rates are at or near their lowest levels in history.

AUGUST 28: I HAVE A DREAM

We will be able to speed up that day when all of God's children, black men and white men, Jews and Gentiles, Protestants and Catholics, will be able to join hands.

~ Martin Luther King ~

On this day in 1963, hundreds of thousands of people watched Martin Luther King deliver his "I Have a Dream" speech in front of the Lincoln Memorial. This famous American oratory was the climax of the momentous March on Washington. In the next year the Civil Rights Act would be signed into law, and the hard work of the Civil Rights Movement would lead to a more just, albeit imperfect, American republic.

THOUGHT FOR TODAY: Improvements in human rights are often the result of peaceful and violent conflict. Martin Luther King made America a better place because of his virtuosic oratory, inspired leadership, and nonviolent methods. America is better thanks to his life and work.

AUGUST 29: MERCANTILISM AND FREE TRADE

The biggest single thing that has lifted people out of poverty is free trade.

~ George Osborne ~

Kings, nobles and aristocrats have always stolen the fruits of labor of the lower classes. Louis XIV's economic advisor Jean-Baptiste Colbert structured the French economy around a principle called mercantilism. Colonies would provide raw materials, and France would trade finished goods with these countries. The policy backfired. Mercantilist policies created a positive balance of trade, but the interstate competition exacerbated by the policy led to many wars, and France's financial position worsened during the height of mercantilism.

THOUGHT FOR TODAY: In the 1700s Adam Smith and others realized the power of free markets to benefit all parties, in contrast to mercantilist policies which brought short-term benefits to the "mother country" but long-term conflict. Today we live in an age of free trade where developing countries grow and poverty rates decline quickly.

AUGUST 30: A VICTOR COMES TO REBUILD, NOT TO HUMILIATE

Build me a son, O Lord, who will be proud and unbending in honest defeat, and humble and gentle in victory.

~ Douglas MacArthur ~

To the victor belong the spoils. This proverb reflects the historically "normal" aftermath of victory. Even as recently as World War I, the victors extracted punitive reparations of Germany, which led to instability and animosity...and another world war.

The United States took a completely different approach after World War II. On this day in 1945, General Douglas Macarthur began his administration of postwar Japan. He came to build a peaceful, democratic Japan. His success exceeded all expectations. Japan became and remains a democratic, prosperous and peaceful nation.

THOUGHT FOR TODAY: Interstate wars and violent conflicts have decreased since World War II. This may be because nations aim to achieve reconciliation after conflict and create paths of peace going forward. The rebuilding of Europe and Japan after World War II demonstrate that the better angels of our nature prevailed.

AUGUST 31: MUSICAL THEATER

I do think there is responsibility to move the musical theater form forward. I think you always have to be aware of the work that came before and build on that.

~ Harold Prince ~

Humans had been performing dramas long before tragedies and comedies were staged in ancient Greece. In the last 100 years a uniquely American genre emerged: musical theater. Pioneers like George Gershwin, Cole Porter, and Richard Rogers shaped the growth of Broadway. Another one of the greats, Alan Jay Lerner, was born on this day in 1918.

Lerner partnered with Frederick Loewe to craft such classics as *Brigadoon, Camelot* and *My Fair Lady*. In the early 1970s Broadway seemed to fizzle, but new shows like *Cats, Les Misérables* and the works of Stephen Sondheim breathed new life into musical theater.

THOUGHT FOR TODAY: Few things change as quickly as popular entertainment. Every time musical theater seems to hit a low, revolutionary musicals like Rent, Avenue Q, and Hamilton come along to inject new life on Broadway.

SEPTEMBER 1: FOUNTAIN OF TIME MARKS 100 YEARS OF PEACE

We are living in a world of beauty, but few of us open our eyes to see it.

~ Lorado Taft ~

Between 1775 and 1814, the US and Great Britain were either locked in war or unsteady peace. The Treaty of Ghent was signed in 1814 in hopes of creating amity between the countries. Few would have imagined that in the ensuing 200 years, the relationship between the US and Britain has been warm and cooperative.

To mark the 100th anniversary of the Treaty of Ghent, the massive sculpture *Fountain of Time* was executed by Lorado Taft in Chicago. It opened on this day in 1920. It depicts a diverse group of one hundred people at various stages of life. It represented a new, more democratic art form.

THOUGHT FOR TODAY: Britain and the US, once enemies, have been friends for more than 200 years. Long periods of peace between nations are becoming more and more common.

SEPTEMBER 2: JOHN HOWARD, PRISON REFORMER

Howard's detailed proposals for improvements were designed to enhance the physical and mental health of the prisoners and the security and order of the prison.

~ Terry Carlson ~

John Howard, born on this day in 1726, grew up in England the son of a well-to-do upholsterer. In early adulthood he was detained by French privateers and spent time in prison. His brief experience behind bars set the course for his future.

Eighteen years later, Howard was appointed High Sheriff of Bedfordshire. When he inspected the county prison, Howard was shocked by the conditions. The next year he went to the House of Commons to testify about prison conditions and made a strong impression on the MPs. Two years later, after inspecting hundreds of prisons, he published *State of the Prisons*, which spurred the British prison reform movement.

THOUGHT FOR TODAY: Prisons were notorious pits of disease, cruelty and deprivation. Through the reforms of people like Howard, prison standards were improved, and the penal systems were professionalized.

SEPTEMBER 3: THE WILDERNESS ACT BECOMES LAW

When we see land as a community to which we belong, we may begin to use it with love and respect.

~ Aldo Leopold ~

Wilderness was once defined as nature that was neglected, abandoned or inhospitable. Land that was not developed for the benefit of humankind was considered a waste of God given resources. But in recent times, wilderness has come to represent wild, beautiful places.

On this day in 1964, President Lyndon Johnson signed the Wilderness Act, which established wild places "where the earth and its community of life are untrammeled by man, where man himself is a visitor who does not remain."

THOUGHT FOR TODAY: Today we have come to appreciate the natural world as it is. We are surrounded by nature that provides solitude for wilderness travel and habitat for plants and animals. And we are finally working to restore wild places to their primeval glory.

SEPTEMBER 4: THE BIRTH OF GOOGLE

Obviously everyone wants to be successful, but I want to be looked back on as being very innovative, very trusted, and ultimately making a big difference in the world.

~ Sergey Brin ~

On this day in 1998, Larry Page and Sergey Brin founded Google. The two Stanford students created an internet company that made its mark with a popular search engine. It would go on to create email, word processing, and many other cloud-based applications.

 **THOUGHT FOR TODAY:** Google offers applications that are essentially free to consumers. These services did not even exist in the 20th century, and they make communication, information management, and many other services easy and accessible.

SEPTEMBER 5: BIRTH OF AN ACTIVIST DYSTOPIAN

Utopias are conceived by optimistic logic which regards constant social and political progress as the ultimate goal of human endeavor.

~ Charles Albert Gobat ~

The 20th century was a time of increased literacy, education and publishing. One popular contemporary genre is dystopian literature. Before 1900, there were just a few dozen dystopian books. Since the turn of the 20th century, at least 200 pieces of major dystopian literature have been written. Classics like *1984, Brave New World,* and *Darkness at Noon* are taught in high school and college. The author of *Darkness at Noon*, Arthur Koestler, was born on this day in 1905. The dystopian world of Communist torture and mind control was washed away by the collapse of communism in the late 1980s.

THOUGHT FOR TODAY: We may fear futures depicted in dystopian literature, but these dark futures haven't come to pass. Despite rampant pessimism, the world has never been richer, more peaceful, and more democratic.

SEPTEMBER 6: REFORMER JANE ADDAMS

Unless our conception of patriotism is progressive, it cannot hope to embody the real affection and the real interest of the nation.

~ Jane Addams ~

On this day in 1860, one of America's great social reformers, Jane Addams, was born. She co-founded Hull House in Chicago, whose mission was "to provide a center for a higher civic and social life and to investigate and improve the conditions in the industrial districts of Chicago." Based on Toynbee House in London (see May 4), Hull House served all kinds of people but was led by women. Addams would also become a prominent peace and women's rights advocate. For her good works she was awarded the Nobel Peace Prize in 1931.

THOUGHT FOR TODAY: Women's reform organizations proliferated during the 19th and 20th century. Besides improving the lives of millions of people, these groups provided leadership opportunities for women as women were finally gaining some measure of legal equality.

SEPTEMBER 7: FIRST PANAMA CANAL TREATY SIGNED

We will demonstrate that as a large and powerful country, we are able to deal fairly and honorably with a proud but smaller sovereign nation.

~ Jimmy Carter ~

On this day in 1977, President Jimmy Carter and Panamanian leader Omar Torrijos signed the first Panama Canal treaty. One hundred years ago, the United States used intrigue and muscle to crowbar Panama from Colombia and then annex the Canal Zone. Jimmy Carter promoted human rights and ethical behavior in America's foreign policy, and he decided to return the Canal Zone to Panama. Many politicians vilified him for giving up this asset, but the transfer has been relatively smooth.

THOUGHT FOR TODAY: We live in a historically unique age of powerful countries giving back ill-gotten gains to weaker ones. If this were done 100 or 1000 years ago, leaders would have scoffed at the soft-heartedness of America's President. Today, doing what is right is part of international relations.

SEPTEMBER 8: A CELEBRATION OF A MAN AND A CIVILIZATION

There is a connection, hard to explain logically but easy to feel, between achievement in public life and progress in the arts.

~ John F. Kennedy ~

John F. Kennedy was president for less than 1000 days but he left an indelible impact on the American imagination. He spoke passionately about the arts. The grandest memorial to his legacy is the Kennedy Center for the Performing Arts in Washington, DC. On this day in 1971, less than 8 years after his assassination, the Kennedy Center opened with a performance of Leonard Bernstein's *Mass*. Since its opening nearly 50 years ago, the Center has hosted thousands of performances, including daily free performances at its Millennium Stage.

THOUGHT FOR TODAY: The accomplishments of civilization are often measured by achievements in war or peace, science or business, but the visual, literary, and performing arts probably say the most about a culture. Both high and popular culture continue to thrive in the 21st century.

SEPTEMBER 9: DEATH OF A DESPOT

Totalitarian regimes had five things in common: a dominant ideology, a single ruling party, a secret police force, a monopoly on information, and a planned economy.

~ Anne Applebaum ~

Communism was a promising idea that ended with the death of millions and the suffering of many more. The Chinese Communists, led by Mao Tse-tung, won a long and hard-fought victory over the corrupt government of Chiang Kai-shek. Nonetheless, the victory was a bitter one for the Chinese people. Among other disasters, Mao engineered the Great Leap Forward and the Cultural Revolution, two social and economic experiments that led to the deaths of millions.

On this day in 1976, Mao Zedong died. Eventually, the pragmatic Deng Xiaoping took over the reins of leadership and led the country to a program of economic liberalization that has made China an economic dynamo.

THOUGHT FOR TODAY: Communism, like fascism, proved to be a disaster, and we are fortunate that only one true Communist totalitarian country—North Korea—still exists.

SEPTEMBER 10: A VERY LARGE LABORATORY GOES ONLINE

There are still many open questions that need to be answered. And the only experiments that can provide answers are those at the Large Hadron Collider.

~ Hubert Kroha ~

Each generation of physicists seems to outdo the previous one. Einstein's Relativity upended the scientific status quo, but the great physicist had a hard time wrapping his mind around quantum mechanics. He derisively quipped "God does not play dice" in reference to this new branch of physics.

Twenty-first century physicists are peeling back the next layer of sub-molecular mysteries at CERN's Large Hadron Collider (LHC), which went online this day in 2008. At the LHC, scientists test different theories about particle physics, including the mysterious Higgs boson.

THOUGHT FOR TODAY: Our understanding of the world at the tiniest and most basic levels continues to grow bigger. Given the track record of the world's great physicists, there is no reason to doubt that many more discovers await.

SEPTEMBER 11: ENERGY EFFICIENT LED LIGHTING

If we all did the things we are really capable of doing, we would literally astound ourselves.

~ Thomas Edison ~

Ever since the incandescent bulb revolutionized lighting, scientists have sought to improve energy efficiency. The first bulbs gave off much light...and too much heat. Fluorescent bulbs proved energy efficient, but many people don't like the light they give off. LED lights were a next breakthrough, but they did not come into widespread use in homes until the 21st century.

On this day in 1960, Japanese scientist Hiroshi Amano was born. Trained as a physicist, he became an inventor of next generation LED lighting technologies and in 2014 was awarded the Nobel Prize, which he shared with Isamu Akasaki and Shuji Nakamura.

THOUGHT FOR TODAY: Lighting technology continues to advance. New bulbs that are brighter, lighter and use less energy have become cheap and commonplace. Today few people need to carry a flashlight because every smartphone has a powerful light.

SEPTEMBER 12: JESSE OWENS' LEGACY

We all have dreams. But in order to make dreams come into reality, it takes an awful lot of determination, dedication, self-discipline, and effort.

~ Jesse Owens ~

Despite often being sick as a child because of chronic lung problems, Jesse Owens became the fastest man alive before he finished college at Ohio State. At the 1936 Olympics he brushed aside Hitler's notions of Aryan superiority when he won four gold medals. Owens, born on this day in 1913, returned home to a racist United States. Nonetheless, by the time he died in 1980, he was a national hero of all Americans, the country he so nobly represented when Hitler's Germany hosted the Olympic Games.

THOUGHT FOR TODAY: Owens proved wrong the racist ideology of Nazi Germany. While racism in America has not been completely wiped out, since Owens' Olympic triumph in 1936, Jim Crow and state-sponsored racism have ended, and the US elected its first black president, Barack Obama.

SEPTEMBER 13: WALTER REED AND MOSQUITO-BORNE ILLNESS

The entire world has benefited since the decisive defeat of Yellow Fever, a far-reaching military victory derived from the field medical discoveries of Walter Reed.

~ *T.K. Naliaka* ~

Yellow fever was once thought to be contracted via foul vapors or unclean water. The real disease vector, mosquitoes, was not surmised until Carlos Finlay studied the disease in his native Cuba and determined that mosquitoes spread the disease. Unfortunately, Finlay's work was largely forgotten until US Army surgeon Walter Reed, born this day in 1851, discovered and built on Finlay's work and disseminated the findings. It led to mosquito suppression, notably during the construction of the Panama Canal, that saved countless lives.

THOUGHT FOR TODAY: The growth of medical knowledge leads to public health policies, preventative programs, and treatments that prevent millions of deaths. Today yellow fever vaccines exist that effectively prevent the disease.

SEPTEMBER 14: HALLELUJAH! HALLELUJAH!

Handel is the greatest and ablest of all composers; from him I can still learn.

~ Beethoven, on his deathbed ~

Music making over the millennia represents some of humanity's greatest inventive output. For reasons both sacred and secular, people sing, drum, blow into instruments, and pluck strings to express emotions, worship gods, and just have fun. On this day in 1741 one of the most beloved compositions of sacred music, Handel's *Messiah*, was completed. For Christians and music lovers of all kinds, the Christmas and Easter performances of this story of Jesus is an aural delight. Each year small performances and sing-alongs take place in addition to the extravaganzas that play the greatest concert halls in the world.

THOUGHT FOR TODAY: Masterpieces like Messiah can be heard on high quality recordings, and live performances of music are abundant as never before. With a performance ticket, internet connection, or smartphone, audiophiles can listen to the greatest music ever created.

SEPTEMBER 15: FIRST FREE SCHOOL FOR THE COMMON FOLK

If from the very earliest years, a child is instructed in both religion and letters, it can be reasonably hoped that his life will be happy.

~ Saint Joseph Calasanz ~

Today we consider a free primary and secondary education a right, but for most of history this was not so. When Joseph of Calasanz opened a free public school for the poor on this day in 1616, it was revolutionary. There were a few contemporaneous schools being set up, but Joseph was such a successful promoter of public education that he was made a saint. He took in Jewish children—uncommon at the time—and even planned to start school in the Ottoman Empire but did not have the teachers to do so.

THOUGHT FOR TODAY: Today we expect that all children should have a free education regardless of their religion or status, but until the recent centuries this was not the norm. Much of our moral and material progress is thanks to increased literacy and education.

SEPTEMBER 16: RELIGIOUS FREEDOM

We must delight in each other, make others conditions our own, rejoice together, mourn together, labor and suffer together.

~ John Winthrop ~

In the 1600s, being a religious nonconformist could get you killed. Much of European history is blighted with religious wars, persecution and witch hunts. On this day in 1620, the Pilgrims left Plymouth, England to find a new home to practice their own religion. In subsequent centuries, waves of Puritans, Jews, Huguenots, Catholics, Mennonites, Quakers and others came to America and other countries to flee persecution.

THOUGHT FOR TODAY: For most of human history, religious nonconformity often led to torture, exile or execution. While some persecution persists, freedom of religion exists in most places and is expanding around the world.

SEPTEMBER 17: GOVERNMENT OF LAWS, NOT MEN

We the People of the United States, in Order to form a more perfect Union, establish Justice, insure domestic Tranquility, provide for the common defense

~ US Constitution ~

On this day in 1787, the US Constitution was signed in Philadelphia. Built upon the English Constitution—and the shortcomings of the Articles of Confederation—the US Constitution created a timeless framework for the rule of law. Many countries have modeled their own constitutions on America's, which has changed surprisingly little over nearly 250 years.

THOUGHT FOR TODAY: Today nearly every country has a codified or implicit constitution, and more than 50 countries celebrate a national Constitution Day. Where once the king or chief ran things with an iron fist, today political leaders are circumscribed by laws, and most of these officials are elected by their citizens.

SEPTEMBER 18: LANDMINE BAN SIGNED

Landmines are different from other conventional weapons. When a war is over, the landmines stay in the ground and continue to kill - for decades.

~ Jody Williams ~

Land mines have been a particularly ugly by-product of modern war. They are indiscriminate; they kill or maim whoever blunders upon them. And in war zones, thousands may remain in the ground after hostilities are over.

At the end of the 20th century, there was a strong push to outlaw the use of landmines. This was one of Princess Diana's causes in the years before she died, and Jody Williams was a principal mover of the work to ban landmines. She and the International Campaign to Ban Landmines were awarded the Nobel Peace Prize in 1997.

THOUGHT FOR TODAY: Use of landmines has declined greatly in recent years. The Canadian Landmine Foundation estimates that tens of thousands of lives and hundreds of thousands of crippling injuries have been prevented because of the anti-landmine treaties of the late 1990s.

SEPTEMBER 19: WOMEN GET THE VOTE IN THE NETHERLANDS

Proof that they do not understand the republic is that in their fine promises for universal suffrage, they forgot women.

~ Delphine de Girardin ~

September marks the anniversary of two dates important in the history of democracy in the Netherlands. On September 18, 1910, 25,000 protesters marched in Amsterdam for the expansion of the vote, which was limited to some men. On September 19, 1919, Dutch women gained the right to vote. In many countries during the early decades of the 20th century, the vote was limited among men, and often only certain men. For example, Southern black Americans could not vote because of discriminatory laws and Jim Crow customs.

 **THOUGHT FOR TODAY:** One hundred years after women started getting the vote, few countries bar voting by sex, race and religion. The 20th century marked the full flowering of the vote for all adults in democracies around the planet.

SEPTEMBER 20: MAGELLAN SETS SAIL

Security is mostly a superstition. Avoiding danger is no safer in the long run than outright exposure. Life is either a daring adventure, or nothing.

~ Helen Keller ~

On this date in 1519, Ferdinand Magellan set sail to circumnavigate the globe. While he and most of his sailors did not survive the voyage, those who pulled into Sanlúcar de Barrameda nearly three years after leaving were the first to circumnavigate the globe. Five hundred years later, anyone can buy a round-the-world airfare for a few thousand dollars and do in two days what Magellan's crew took three years to complete.

THOUGHT FOR TODAY: The explorations of the early modern period brought the world together, both for good and ill. Today world commerce and travel have led to a globally cosmopolitan civilization where countries and people borrow, influence, trade and cooperate.

SEPTEMBER 21: THE FIRST FEMALE SUPREME COURT JUSTICE

We don't accomplish anything in this world alone and whatever happens is the result of the whole tapestry of one's life and all the weavings of individual threads.

~ Sandra Day O'Connor ~

In 1981 the US Senate unanimously voted for Sandra Day O'Connor to be the first female justice on the Supreme Court. Thirty-five years later, three of the nine justices are women. In 2016, for the first time ever in the US, women made up the majority of students in law schools.

 **THOUGHT FOR TODAY:** While gender parity progress has been slow, it has been accelerating in recent decades. Education rates for girls are nearing those for boys, which means the future workforce will be more balanced by sex. Women are common in most professions, and more than a dozen national governments are led by female presidents or prime ministers.

SEPTEMBER 22: THE EMANCIPATION PROCLAMATION

A house divided against itself cannot stand. I believe this government cannot endure permanently half-slave and half-free.

~ Abraham Lincoln ~

Jesus often talked about slavery in the New Testament, but he never suggested it be ended. This demonstrated how slavery was an accepted institution in the ancient world. Over the centuries, those in power saw themselves in the faces of the enslaved. On this day in 1862, after the Union victory at Antietam, Abraham Lincoln drafted the Emancipation Proclamation, which on January 1, 1863, was formally promulgated.

THOUGHT FOR TODAY: While the Emancipation Proclamation freed no slaves, it made clear that the Civil War was about reuniting the country and freeing the enslaved. Slavery was ended after the Civil War when the 13th Amendment to the Constitution was ratified.

SEPTEMBER 23: FIRST COMMENCEMENT CEREMONIES AT HARVARD

Education is the most powerful weapon which you can use to change the world.

~ Nelson Mandela ~

In 1642 Harvard College, America's first school for higher learning, graduated nine students. Now Harvard graduates thousands of students every year. And thousands of other universities graduate thousands of their own students. The university is one of the great "inventions" of the Middle Ages, and widespread access to college education has transformed the world.

THOUGHT FOR TODAY: While much inequality to education access remains, barriers are falling, and students rich and poor, male and female, of all races are earning bachelor's, master's, and doctoral degrees. (Liz Murray, whose birthday is today, is known as the woman who went "from homeless to Harvard.") Today Harvard's president is female, as are the presidents of three other Ivies (Penn, Brown and Cornell).

SEPTEMBER 24: COMPREHENSIVE NUCLEAR TEST BAN IS SIGNED

In terms of weapons, the best disarmament tool so far is nuclear energy. We have been taking down the Russian warheads, turning it into electricity.

~ Stewart Brand ~

The best thing about nuclear weapons is that we haven't used them for more than 70 years. After the end of the Cold War, thousands of nuclear weapons were decommissioned and turned into fuel for nuclear power plants. A regime of international agreements, including the Comprehensive Test Ban Treaty (CTBT), have been created to deter nuclear proliferation. One of the best outcomes of the CTBT is a system of more than 300 monitoring stations to detect nuclear tests.

THOUGHT FOR TODAY: A comprehensive web of international agreements have cemented a more peaceful world order. International cooperation means that major power conflicts rarely erupt into war, and treaties like the Nuclear Test Ban, which was signed by the US on this day in 1996, have made major power nuclear war highly unlikely.

SEPTEMBER 25: CENTRAL HIGH IN LITTLE ROCK IS INTEGRATED

The arc of the moral universe is long, but it bends toward justice

*~ **Martin Luther King** ~*

Despite the resistance of local and state officials, notably governor Orval Faubus, Central High School in Little Rock, Arkansas was integrated by force of law and federal troops. The first nine black students at Central High School lived through a year of icy ostracism amid halls monitored by federal troops. Their brave pioneering effort was another blow to Jim Crow and racism in America.

THOUGHT FOR TODAY: Today, state-sponsored segregation that was a hallmark of the 1950s seems unthinkable, especially in the wake of the presidency of Barack Obama. But such segregation, be it Jim Crow in the United States or the caste system in India, was once the norm across cultures and around the world.

SEPTEMBER 26: EINSTEIN PUBLISHES FIRST PAPER ON RELATIVITY

Strive not to be a success, but rather to be of value.

~ Albert Einstein ~

Einstein upended Newtonian physics with his theory of relativity. His first paper on this topic was published on this day in 1905. Scientific revolutions since this paper have occurred at an ever-accelerating pace. It took hundreds of years for Einstein to challenge Newtonian physics. In Einstein's own lifetime the revolution of quantum mechanics baffled the genius of Princeton.

THOUGHT FOR TODAY: Scientific revolutions can feel disruptive, but these disruptions show that scientists are building a more comprehensive understanding of our infinite—and infinitely fascinating—universe.

SEPTEMBER 27: PRODUCTION OF THE FORD MODEL T BEGINS

If I had asked people what they wanted, they would have said faster horses.

~ Henry Ford ~

In 1908, Ford Motor Company began production of the first car build for the mass market, the Model T. With the onset of the automobile came a revolution in America and the world. The thousands of tons of horse manure that befouled the streets would become a thing of the past. Rail had connected cities and towns, but the Model T meant middle class and rural folk could drive from their farm to the big city or anywhere they pleased.

THOUGHT FOR TODAY: Ford would also revolutionize work in factories. In the years following the rollout of the Model T, he would institute 40-hour work weeks and double the pay of assembly line workers. Industrialization was critiqued as alienating and bad for workers, but instead it led to shorter work weeks, more affluence, and social mobility.

SEPTEMBER 28: ALEXANDER FLEMING NOTICES SOME UNUSUAL MOLD

When I woke up just after dawn on September 28, 1928, I certainly didn't plan to revolutionise all medicine by discovering the world's first antibiotic.

~ Alexander Fleming ~

Like many scientific breakthroughs, the discovery of penicillin was an accident. Alexander Fleming often left his laboratory in an untidy condition, and this was the case when he stacked cultures of staphylococci one day. On the morning of September 28, he was befuddled when he found a mold had infected and killed some staphylococci. This led him to intensively study what would become penicillin, the first antibiotic. By the end of World War II, penicillin saved thousands of lives. Fleming was awarded the Nobel Prize in 1945 for his discovery of antibiotics, disease-fighters that are now ubiquitous.

THOUGHT FOR TODAY: Today we have a bevy of antibiotics that effectively treat most bacterial diseases. The antibiotics pioneered by Fleming may have saved more than a billion lives.

SEPTEMBER 29: FIRST PUBLIC ELECTRIC TRAMWAY OPENED

All travel has its advantages. If the passenger visits better countries, he may learn to improve his own. And if fortune carries him to worse, he may learn to enjoy it.

~ *Samuel Johnson* ~

In ancient times there were few public conveyances, save the occasional ferry. Canal boats became available to the public, notably in ancient China and early modern Europe. Stagecoaches date from at least the 13th century in England. The introduction of the omnibus in Paris in 1662 was a failure, but the idea survived in Nantes, and by the 1800s buses started running in London and other cities.

THOUGHT FOR TODAY: With the invention of steam locomotives, speedy travel become available to a much wider segment of the population. On September 29, 1885, the Blackpool Tramway opened, ushering in a new form of mass transit to the world.

SEPTEMBER 30: THE DEBUT OF THE MAGIC FLUTE

Mozart was one of the greatest successes we know of, a man who in his early thirties had poured out his inexhaustible gift of music, leaving the world richer.

~ Eleanor Roosevelt ~

On this day in 1791, Mozart's last opera, *The Magic Flute*, debuted just two months before his death. More than 225 years later, it remains one of the most popular operas of all time (and Mozart's most performed). Great civilizations often lose their treasures with the passage of time, but the gems of European classical music have been preserved and are widely performed hundreds of years later.

 **THOUGHT FOR TODAY:** Today we can enjoy recordings of most of Mozart's 600 works, and his compositions are heard in many places around the world every day. The preservation of such works of genius is something for which we should feel very fortunate.

OCTOBER 1: NAZI LEADERS SENTENCED AT NUREMBERG

The clearest way to show what the rule of law means to us in everyday life is to recall what has happened when there is no rule of law.

~ Dwight D. Eisenhower ~

The Nuremberg Trials were held in Germany after World War II to force a public accounting, trial and punishment of Nazi atrocities. On this day in 1946, 20 leading Nazis were handed sentences of death or imprisonment for crimes against humanity. At that time, the idea of international courts was fairly new in world history.

 **THOUGHT FOR TODAY:** The Nuremberg Trials became a template for future legal actions in cases of war crimes, crimes against humanity, and wars of aggression. Today, thanks to precursors like the Nuremberg Trials, there is a system of international adjudication for conflicts and crimes, including the International Court of Justice at the Hague.

OCTOBER 2: THURGOOD MARSHALL IS SWORN IN

None of us got where we are solely by pulling ourselves up by our bootstraps. We got here because somebody bent down and helped us pick up our boots.

~ Thurgood Marshall ~

The first African-American justice of the Supreme Court was sworn in on this day in 1967. Thirteen years before being sworn in, Marshall was the lead attorney who argued against segregation in the landmark Brown vs. Board of Education case. His switch from insurgent upending a racist system to justice of the highest court in the land demonstrated the rapid, if tragically belated, improvements in civil rights in the mid-20th century.

THOUGHT FOR TODAY: The Supreme Court, once a white Anglo-Saxon Protestant bastion like much of the upper echelons of American society, now includes whites and blacks, men and women, Jews and gentiles.

OCTOBER 3: GERMANY IS REUNIFIED

With the end of the Cold War, all the 'isms' of the 20th century - Fascism, Nazism, Communism and the evil of apartheid-ism - have failed.

~ Jack Kemp ~

For Baby Boomers, the Cold War was a fact of life. Before the late 1980s, few imagined that the Soviet Union and its satellite states would dissolve and the East-West nuclear deadlock that marred life in the 50s, 60s, 70s and 80s would come to an end. But end it did, and in spectacular form. Today most of the Eastern European countries that were Soviet satellites are now democracies with modern economies.

THOUGHT FOR TODAY: Near the end of the 20th century, the Berlin Wall and Iron Curtain fell. Germany reunified and eastern Germany has largely caught up with its western counterpart. It is easy to forget how the end of Communism transformed the world for the better.

OCTOBER 4: SPUTNIK (AND THE SPACE AGE) IS LAUNCHED

We cannot predict the new forces, powers, and discoveries that will be disclosed to us when we reach the other planets and set up new laboratories in space.

~ Arthur C. Clarke ~

On this day in 1957, the world changed when the Soviet Union launched the first satellite into space. Since Sputnik 1 was sent into orbit, more than 40 countries have launched some 6500 satellites into space. Use of satellites has revolutionized television, communications, weather, astronomy and navigation.

THOUGHT FOR TODAY: When Sputnik sailed into space, people feared nuclear bombs would fall from the sky. Instead of delivering terror from above, satellites and space exploration have enriched our lives. Astronauts and Cosmonauts—once Cold War adversaries—now cooperate at the International Space Station, where there is a constant human presence in space.

OCTOBER 5: DENIS DIDEROT, CHAMPION OF HUMAN KNOWLEDGE

We swallow greedily any lie that flatters us, but we sip only little by little at a truth we find bitter.

~ Denis Diderot ~

During the Enlightenment, French *philosophes* collaborated on the *Encyclopédie*. It became a compendium of enlightenment thought in a time when philosophers and scientists wanted to capture and disseminate knowledge for the betterment of humanity. Today billions of people have the accumulated knowledge of humankind at their fingertips thanks to computers and the internet.

Denis Diderot, who was a founder, chief editor, and contributor to the Encyclopédie, was born today. His project to disseminate human knowledge has mushroomed a thousandfold in the 21st century.

THOUGHT FOR TODAY: When you browse the internet, open Wikipedia and take a look at all the topics. There are more than five million English language entries in Wikipedia, and the free encyclopedia expands every day. Wikipedia is a just a tiny part of the information explosion happening on the internet.

OCTOBER 6: BEN FRANKLIN ARRIVES IN PHILADELPHIA

Either write something worth reading or do something worth writing.

~ Benjamin Franklin ~

October 6 marks two important occasions for American bibliophiles. In 1723, Benjamin Franklin arrived in Philadelphia. Eight years later he and a group of friends founded America's first membership library. Nearly 60 years later he donated his personal library to a town in Massachusetts and this collection became the first American public library.

In 1876, the American Library Association (ALA) was formed. The ALA has played a role in expanding and improving American libraries, both public and private. Today nearly every community has a public library, a fact that reflects widespread literacy and the triumph of education.

THOUGHT FOR TODAY: When you pass a library, remember that free and accessible books are a relatively new innovation. In more and more places in the world, libraries offer a quiet space to read, learn, study and enjoy literature.

OCTOBER 7: MOTHER TERESA BEGINS HER WORK

If we have no peace, it is because we have forgotten that we belong to each other.

~ Mother Teresa ~

On this day Mother Teresa created the Missionaries of Charity to care for, in her words, "the hungry, the naked, the homeless, the crippled, the blind, the lepers, all those people who feel unwanted, unloved, uncared for throughout society, people that have become a burden to the society and are shunned by everyone."

Today the Missionaries of Charity have 19 centers in Calcutta with some 4500 Sisters of Charity in the order she formed. Mother Teresa is now Saint Teresa of Calcutta, a role model of someone who dedicates her life to the most destitute. Her work lives on.

THOUGHT FOR TODAY: When you pass a food bank, a clinic, or a nonprofit community organization, consider the explosion of relief organizations that have proliferated in the last century.

OCTOBER 8: SOLZHENITSYN WINS NOBEL PRIZE FOR LITERATURE

The battle line between good and evil runs through the heart of every man.

~ Alexander Solzhenitsyn ~

In 1970, Alexander Solzhenitsyn seemed to be a lonely voice writing in protest against the Soviet Union. In works like *The Gulag Archipelago*, he exposed the oppression of the Soviet Union. He would outlive the USSR by more than 15 years.

George Kennan, the architect of America's containment policy to oppose the Soviet Union, said that *Gulag* was "the greatest and most powerful single indictment of a political regime ever to be leveled in modern times."

THOUGHT FOR TODAY: Under Vladimir Putin, Russia has returned to some of its authoritarian ways but not its totalitarian extremes. Life around the world has been much better—and freer—since the fall of Communism, a goal championed by author-activists like Alexander Solzhenitsyn.

OCTOBER 9: ROGER WILLIAMS BANISHED!

The greatest crime is not developing your potential. When you do what you do best, you are helping not only yourself, but the world.

~ Roger Williams ~

Religious orthodoxy was demanded by tribes, cities, and nations for most of history. Even liberal Athens was prone to intolerance. Socrates was accused "of believing in deities of his own invention instead of the gods recognized by the city."

Nonetheless, the modern period has seen more religious freedom and tolerance. On this date in 1635, Roger Williams was banished from Massachusetts Bay Colony because of his unorthodox beliefs. He moved south and became one of the leaders of Rhode Island. The new colony became a safe haven for religious refugees, including persecuted Jews, who founded the first synagogue in America in Newport, Rhode Island.

 **THOUGHT FOR TODAY:** Freedom of religion is guaranteed by the US Constitution, and today freedom of religion is the norm in most places around the world.

OCTOBER 10: OUTER SPACE TREATY ENTERS INTO FORCE

Our passionate preoccupation with the sky, the stars, and a God somewhere in outer space is a homing impulse. We are drawn back to where we came from.

~ Eric Hoffer ~

For most of history, explorers and armies conquered faraway lands and claimed them for crown and country. In the mid-1960s, the Outer Space Treaty was drafted and signed as the legal framework of international space law. It bars countries from placing weapons of mass destruction in orbit around Earth or on the Moon. The treaty states that celestial bodies should be used for peaceful purposes and prohibits their militarization. The UN Committee on the Peaceful Uses of Outer Space (COPUOS) overseas the treaty.

THOUGHT FOR TODAY: In recent years, many countries have shown a reluctance to support international agreements. This short-sighted trend ignores the peace and progress fostered by the many interconnecting international agreements that have made cooperation more common and conflict less so.

OCTOBER 11: SATURDAY NIGHT LIVE DEBUTS

If you work for Second City, there's an audience, and you die in the improv set five times out of nine. And Saturday Night Live was as tough as Second City.

~ Bill Murray ~

In the 90s, the stand-up comedy scene centered on small clubs. Today the number and size of comedy venues continues increasing. The growth of comedy can be traced in part to the debut of *Saturday Night Live (SNL)* on this day in 1975. At first the show had a small cult following. Forty-two years later *SNL* is an institution. It launched or accelerated the careers of John Belushi, Gilda Radner, Bill Murray, Tina Fey, Will Ferrell, and Amy Poehler, to name a few.

 **THOUGHT FOR TODAY:** According to industry insider Nick Nuciforo, "There are more comedians right now playing the 1,000-plus seat theaters than ever." Comedy is available on Sirius XM, Comedy Central, and on the web. We live in a golden age of comedy.

OCTOBER 12: THE FIRST OKTOBERFEST IN MUNICH

If bread is the staff of life, then beer is life itself.

~ English proverb ~

On this date in 1810, Crown Prince Ludwig wed Princess Therese. The public was invited to celebrate with horse races, citizen performances, and beer and wine tastings. This celebration grew into Oktoberfest, the annual massive Munich beer fest. Today the festival is in September, and some two-million gallons of beer are consumed over a two-and-a-half-week period.

THOUGHT FOR TODAY: We live in something of a beer Renaissance in the 21st century. The United States, once considered a beer wasteland, now has some 5000 breweries. Ninety-nine percent of these are privately owned. Whether you prefer ale, amber, bock, bitter, IPA, lager, pilsner, porter, stout or weiss-bier, your beer has never been better.

OCTOBER 13: THE PRIME MERIDIAN IS DETERMINED

Anytime I feel lost, I pull out a map and stare. I stare until I have reminded myself that life is a giant adventure, so much to do, to see.

~ Angelina Jolie ~

It's fun to look at old maps with their speculative drawings of faraway continents, terra incognito, and "there be monsters here" warnings. By the time Chester Arthur called for the International Meridian Conference in 1884, the world had been thoroughly explored. International trade and travel were getting more complex, and cooperation to encourage safe and accurate navigation was needed. Delegates from 26 nations met to determine "a meridian to be employed as a common zero of longitude." It was determined that the Royal Observatory Greenwich east of London would determine the Prime Meridian for longitude, and that time would be standardized from Greenwich as well. Eventually nearly every country adopted this standard for navigation and time.

THOUGHT FOR TODAY: The International Meridian Conference was another progressive step toward world integration and cooperation.

OCTOBER 14: FIRST GAY RIGHTS MARCH ON WASHINGTON

There is a fantasy that if all our skins turned lavender overnight, the majority, confounded by our numbers, would at once let go of prejudice forevermore.

~ Ian McKellen ~

On this day in 1979, 100,000 people marched on Washington to demand equal rights for Lesbian, Gay, Bisexual and Transgender (LGBT) Americans. The catalyst for the march was the assassination of politician Harvey Milk (see May 22), a tragedy that galvanized the activists. The 1979 march would also commemorate the 10th anniversary of the Stonewall riots (see June 28). The protesters marched for civil rights protections, an end to government discrimination, the repeal of all anti-LGBT laws, and legal protection for LGBT parents and children.

 **THOUGHT FOR TODAY:** In the past few years, LGBT Americans have been gaining more and more rights. While a minority of Americans still resist full equality of LGBTs, marriage is now legal for all couples regardless of sexual orientation.

OCTOBER 15: FIRST ASCENT IN A HOT AIR BALLOON

For once you have tasted flight you will walk the earth with your eyes turned skywards, for there you have been and there you will long to return.

~ Leonardo da Vinci ~

On this day in 1783, Jean-François Pilâtre de Rozier piloted the first balloon flight with a human passenger. The balloon was designed by French inventors, the brothers Joseph-Michel and Jacques-Étienne Montgolfier. In the following century balloon innovations continued, but it was fixed winged flight invented by another pair of brothers—Wilbur and Orville Wright—that revolutionized air travel. Now balloons are mostly used for recreation and weather, but every day airplanes take millions of travelers all over the planet.

 **THOUGHT FOR TODAY:** Since earliest times, humans looked up at the birds and butterflies in envy. When you see an airplane overhead, remind yourself how incredible flight is. Only in recent decades has air travel opened up to much of the population. Today, more than a billion people have flown in an airplane.

OCTOBER 16: MARGARET SANGER OPENS FIRST BIRTH CONTROL CLINIC

Margaret Sanger didn't just introduce the idea of birth control into our culture at large, she freed women from indenture to their bodies.

~ Roxane Gay ~

Until modern times, men controlled women's reproductive choices. But around the time that women gained the vote, Margaret Sanger opened the first birth control clinic for women in the US. Sanger was arrested and tried for distributing information about contraception. On appeal a judge ruled that contraception could be prescribed by a doctor, and slowly access opened for women.

She tirelessly campaigned to make contraception available. Today most women have access to birth control, including 300 million in the developing world. Because of this, and rising wealth and declining poverty, birth rates are falling all over the world.

 **THOUGHT FOR TODAY:** Contraception access for woman has slowed population growth, strengthened women's rights, and allowed men and women to enjoy the well-being and relational joys of sex with greater freedom.

OCTOBER 17: EDISON'S MOVING PICTURE MACHINE

I am experimenting upon an instrument which does for the Eye what the phonograph does for the Ear.

~ Thomas Edison ~

On this day in 1894, Thomas Edison's Kinetoscopes were set up for public use in London. This novelty was an early "peephole" motion picture device. Projection machines were developed in the late 1800s, and by the early 1900s the movie business was expanding.

Today anyone with a smartphone can take movies much better than the ones first developed by Edison and other inventors, and these images can be shared around the world.

THOUGHT FOR TODAY: When you watch a video—on your phone, on TV, or at the movies—remind yourself that this technology is quite new. What would life be like without the movies? No Wizard of Oz, Forrest Gump, and On the Waterfront? The quantity and quality of entertainment has never been better.

OCTOBER 18: THE FIRST TRANSISTOR RADIO

The transistor was a small plastic unit that would take us from a world of static bricks piled on top of each other to a world where everything was interactive.

~ Ayah Bdeir ~

On this day in 1954, Texas Instruments introduced the first transistor radio. By the end of the 1960s, billions of transistor radios had been manufactured, making them one of the most popular electronics devices of all time. These portable radios meant entertainment was available on the go. All over the globe, people were exposed to music, news, and culture.

Radio provided the soundtrack for many young people. What songs remind you of the best years of your life? If you listen to radio, what are your favorite stations and programs?

 **THOUGHT FOR TODAY:** When you hear the radio, remember that it didn't exist 100 years ago. Transistor radios ushered in an age of smaller audio players with more capabilities. Nowadays you can listen to thousands of stations for free via the internet.

OCTOBER 19: BETTER, BRIGHTER TEETH

You don't have to brush all your teeth, just the ones you want to keep.

~ Anonymous ~

One stereotype of Americans is that they have good teeth. In recent years, everybody else has been catching up. This is due to better nutrition and health care in general, but also improved dental care. Regular cleaning and checkups are becoming the norm in wealthy countries.

This improvement is reflected in decayed, missing, and filled teeth (DMFT) statistics. As of 1980, 12-year-olds in many wealthy countries had, on average, four to nine DMFTs. Today these averages are down to one and two DMFTs. This is good news because people are living longer, and they'll want their teeth to last a long time.

THOUGHT FOR TODAY: Progress in dental care in the last half century has been remarkable. In the late 1950s, more than two-thirds of elderly Americans experienced tooth loss. Today, fewer than one-quarter of them lose teeth.

OCTOBER 20: FIRST EDITION OF A GREAT NEWSPAPER

Were it left to me to decide whether we should have government without newspapers or newspapers without government, I should not hesitate to prefer the latter.

~Thomas Jefferson~

The newspaper as we know it started as handwritten news sheets in Venice in the mid-16th century. The first printed paper followed in around 1600. Early newspapers were heavily censored, but over the course of the 17th and 18th centuries, censorship relaxed. On this day in 1822, the first edition of the *Sunday Times* was published in London.

In the 1800s, tabloids and broadsheets proliferated in cities big and small. And in the last century, journalism in its many forms has brought current affairs to everyone.

 **THOUGHT FOR TODAY:** Today journalism thrives even as the internet has thrown traditional outlets into uncertainty. Despite major changes in the news business, institutions like the Sunday Times and The New York Times are still going strong.

OCTOBER 21: FLORENCE NIGHTINGALE LEAVES FOR THE CRIMEA

I attribute my success to this - I never gave or took any excuse.

~ Florence Nightingale ~

On this day in 1865, "The Lady with the Lamp" left Britain with 54 nurses for the Crimea. Florence Nightingale, as a leader of nurses during the Crimean War, would pioneer the professionalization of the nursing profession. Her accomplishments were all the more revolutionary given the circumscribed roles of women in the mid-1800s. After the war, Nightingale went on to establish the first secular nursing school, and she drafted the "Nightingale Pledge," a Hippocratic Oath for nurses.

THOUGHT FOR TODAY: Like many of the great women of her era, Nightingale was a social reformer in several areas, including hunger, healthcare and women's rights. Her legacy is the modern nursing profession, the backbone of our healthcare system.

OCTOBER 22: THE GREAT ANTICIPATION IS A DISAPPOINTMENT

Once we start believing that the apocalypse is coming, (the brain) goes on high alert, filtering out most anything that says otherwise.

~ Peter Diamandis ~

One of the most important concepts in psychology is the negativity bias. For good evolutionary reasons, humans anticipate, perceive, think about, and worry over worst-case scenarios much more often than they see goodness and opportunity. There is no better example of this psychological trait than the persistence of end-of-the-world predictions and preparations.

On this day in 1844, preacher William Miller predicted the end of the world. When nothing happened, his Great Anticipation became the Great Disappointment. These predictions seem more a part of the human psyche than real threats. Most recently, David Meade predicted the end of the world on September 23, 2017. Once again, the world did not end.

THOUGHT FOR TODAY: Many hundreds of apocalypses have been predicted but none have occurred. Perhaps pessimism is an unrealistic distortion of the world and the human condition.

OCTOBER 23: UN GENERAL ASSEMBLY CONVENES FOR THE FIRST TIME

The UN acts as the world's conscience, and over 85% percent of the work that is done by the United Nations is in the social, economic, educational and cultural fields.

~ Shirley Temple ~

On this day in 1946, the United Nations (UN) General Assembly met for the first time in Flushing, New York. It would move to its permanent headquarters on the East River in New York City in October of 1952.

The world body is accused of being ineffective and bloated, but the UN has had many successes. It is a world headquarters where diplomats work together. Many initiatives have been monumental successes, like the World Health Organization's leadership in the eradication of smallpox (see May 8), the Montreal Protocols to fix the ozone hole (see January 1), and the role of UNICEF in saving children's lives (see December 11).

THOUGHT FOR TODAY: The UN has played an important role in making our world safer and healthier. Cooperation has meant more peace, less war, and greater well-being.

OCTOBER 24: THE PEACE OF WESTPHALIA

The Westphalia peace relied on a system of independent states refraining from interfering in each other's domestic affairs and checking each other's ambitions.

~ Henry Kissinger ~

The Thirty Years War was one of Europe's many paroxysms of violence. The Peace of Westphalia, the agreement that ended the war, was signed on this day in 1648. The Peace created a doctrine of state sovereignty still in force today, as well as a model for multi-state peace conferences.

In the 21st century, demagogues and dictators have scoffed at the web of international agreements that keep the peace. While treaties limit the power of states to act independently, this constraint makes it much more difficult for countries to invade their neighbors or mettle in their affairs.

THOUGHT FOR TODAY: Our age is one of unprecedented global cooperation, which has led to more peace. This new peace allows us to focus on ending poverty, improving education, and making the lives of citizens better in many different ways.

OCTOBER 25: ENGLISH BOWMEN LEVEL THE PLAYING FIELD

We few, we happy few, we band of brothers; for he to-day
that sheds his blood with me shall be my brother

~ William Shakespeare, Henry V's speech at Agincourt ~

On this day in 1415, English peasants beat French knights at the Battle of Agincourt. During the Middle Ages, the mounted knight was considered the ultimate weapon, but English victories at Crécy, Poitiers and Agincourt heralded the rise of peasant infantry. Less than 100 years after Agincourt, at the Battle of Cerignola (1503), artillery and arquebuses (early firearms) heralded the coming of modern warfare and the end of noble combat.

 **THOUGHT FOR TODAY:** In The Iliad and other ancient epics, noble warriors determined the fate of nations. The fall of the armored nobleman and the rise of citizen infantry was another demonstration of the basic equality of all people, and a starting point for democracy.

OCTOBER 26: DISRUPTIVE TECHNOLOGIES, CIRCA 1860

Modernity is disruptive, and I endorse that.

~ Emmanuel Macron ~

On this day the famed Pony Express went out of business. The Express was a romantic idea inspired by a real need for fast coast-to-coast communications in the US. William Russell, Alexander Majors, and William Waddell founded the Pony Express to deliver letters between St. Joseph, Missouri and Sacramento, California. While the Express delivered some 35,000 pieces of mail, it was made obsolete after two years of business when a transcontinental telegraph line connected the coasts.

 **THOUGHT FOR TODAY:** We often think we live in a time uniquely affected by disruptive technologies, but ever since humans smelted bronze, disruptive technologies have spelled doom to older ways. Technological disruption is not a threat; it's what we humans do, and we do it to make life better.

OCTOBER 27: FIRST NEW YORK CITY SUBWAY LINE OPENS

New York, New York, a wonderful town

The Bronx is up and the Battery's down

The people ride in a hole in the ground

~ Betty Comden and Adolph Green ~

On this day in 1904, the IRT Line between City Hall and 125th Street opened in New York City. Until the 1800s, mass transit did not exist at a scale to serve all citizens, rich and poor. Big city subways made travel much easier, and today there are more than a hundred big city metro systems around the world. Right now, there is a subway building boom in China and India, countries that have become much more prosperous in recent decades. These massive transportation systems are eco-friendly and make living in cities much more convenient.

 **THOUGHT FOR TODAY:** Mass transit is an efficient way to transport people around the bustling metropolises of modern life. It gives transport power to the people and is much greener than commuting via automobile.

OCTOBER 28: ELVIS GETS VACCINATED

Parents whose children are vaccinated no longer have to worry about their child's death from whooping cough, polio, diphtheria, hepatitis, or a host of other infections.

~ Ezekiel Emanuel ~

On this day in 1956, superstar Elvis Presley got a polio shot on The Ed Sullivan Show. Dr. Leona Baumgartner had blitzed the print, radio and TV media with medical facts and promotions to get people to get their polio shots, but it was unsuccessful. When she enlisted Elvis Presley to get a polio shot on the Ed Sullivan show, vaccinations rates went up to 80% within six months. Some have argued that Elvis' promotion of the polio vaccine may have been one of the most effective public health promotions of all time.

THOUGHT FOR TODAY: Reflect on all the vaccinations you received throughout your life. These simple public health interventions save millions of lives each year...and they may have saved yours. Today polio is very close to eradication thanks to people like Jonas Salk, Leona Baumgartner...and Elvis.

OCTOBER 29: THE RED CROSS IS CREATED

The Red Cross in its nature is unlike any other organization. It cannot await the ordinary deliberation of organized bodies if it would be of use to suffering humanity.

~ Clara Barton ~

For nearly all of history, humanitarian aid in response to disasters was a haphazard affair. On October 29, 1863, delegations from 12 European principalities passed resolutions that created national relief societies for wounded soldiers, use of volunteer forces for relief on the battlefield, and the introduction of the distinctive Red Cross symbol for medical personnel in the field.

The Red Cross would go on to become a first responder for disasters of all kinds. Today death rates from natural disasters have never been lower, thanks in part to the work started 150 years ago by the Red Cross.

THOUGHT FOR TODAY: Until the 1800s, there were no organizations that could effectively respond to humanitarian crises. Today, thousands of organizations, both public and private, prevent deaths, treat victims, and aid recovery from natural disasters.

OCTOBER 30: GATT IS SIGNED

Capitalism is a dirty word for many intellectuals, but there are studies showing that open economies and free trade are negatively correlated with genocide and war.

~ Steven Pinker ~

The Great Depression was characterized by stagnant economies and weak international trade. Since World War II, the world economy has grown explosively thanks to reduced trade barriers.

On this day in 1947, the General Agreement on Tariffs and Trade (GATT) was signed. This agreement created a framework that evolved into the World Trade Organization (WTO). Protests against the WTO made headlines, but now experts believe that trade facilitated by the WTO lifted hundreds of millions of people out of abject poverty in China and India.

THOUGHT FOR TODAY: World trade is often vilified as the cause of job losses, but globalization caused the greatest decrease in poverty ever. In 2018, despite complaints by some that free trade leads to job losses in the US, the American economy is near full employment.

OCTOBER 31: THE PROTESTANT REFORMATION BEGINS

The Reformer is always right about what's wrong. However, he's often wrong about what is right.

~ G.K. Chesterton ~

On this day in 1517, Martin Luther tacked his 95 theses to the church door in Wittenberg. This act changed Europe forever, for worse and better. It began the Reformation, which included more than 100 years of religious wars, some of the bloodiest in history. Luther also was an anti-Semite. But he also empowered every Christian to become literate and interpret the Bible for him or herself.

 **THOUGHT FOR TODAY:** The Protestant Reformation provides cautionary lessons about how faith can divide us and the hypocrisy of religious war. It also empowered individuals to find God on their own terms through literacy. The Protestant emphasis on reading may have been the greatest literacy promotion program in history, which took place in tandem with the rise of the printing press.

NOVEMBER 1: WILLIAM LEAVES HOLLAND FOR ENGLAND

You can never have a revolution in order to establish a democracy. You must have a democracy in order to have a revolution.

~ *G. K. Chesterton* ~

On this day in 1688, a Dutch fleet left the Netherlands to conquer England. The successful invasion led to The Glorious Revolution, a relatively bloodless overthrow of the Stuart Dynasty by William and Mary. The most important outcome was the creation of a constitutional monarchy that expanded the power of Parliament and led to the English Bill of Rights.

The Glorious Revolution marked a shift from violent succession struggles toward bloodless transitions of power. Eventually, representative democracy would develop, today the most common form of government.

 **THOUGHT FOR TODAY:** Even small limits on a monarch were revolutionary in 1688, and now the rule of law limits the abuse of power in all democratic governments. Democracy is a blessing that was won by our forebears, but its triumph is never guaranteed forever. Eternal vigilance is the price of liberty.

NOVEMBER 2: PRESIDENT KENNEDY PROPOSES THE PEACE CORPS

The Peace Corps is guilty of enthusiasm and a crusading spirit. But we're not apologetic about it.

~ Sargent Shriver ~

On the campaign trail a few days before the presidential election, John F. Kennedy proposed "a peace corps of talented men and women." His proposal became reality a year later. Fifty years after the founding of the Peace Corps, some 200,000 American have served in over 140 countries.

It is now commonplace for countries to send skilled technicians and teachers to aid development in foreign lands. Trust between nations has grown such that it is cooperation, not bellicose competition, that characterizes most of the interaction between countries. Kennedy's Peace Corps is but one manifestation of humankind's increasing cooperation.

THOUGHT FOR TODAY: For most of history, countries invaded their neighbors. Since the mid-20th century, rich countries have started helping developing countries to alleviate poverty, improve education, and increase living standards.

NOVEMBER 3: THE EMPEROR ASSENTS TO A NEW CONSTITUTION

Democracy alone, of all forms of government, enlists the full force of men's enlightened will.

~ Franklin D. Roosevelt ~

During the first half of the 20th century, Japan's hyper-nationalistic militarism blazed a swath of destruction throughout East Asia. After it capitulated to the Allies, the country made an about-face and became a constitutional monarchy wherein the Emperor became a figurehead with no political power.

The transformation of Germany and Japan from aggressors to peaceful members of the United Nations was amazing in its swiftness. This shift from militarism to membership in the global community exemplifies the decrease in war and increase in democracy and freedom that characterizes our times, especially since the fall of Communism.

THOUGHT FOR TODAY: For most of history leaders ruled according to their own desires and whims. Today, rule of law and not of men is the new norm.

NOVEMBER 4: BARACK OBAMA IS ELECTED PRESIDENT

Change will not come if we wait for some other person or some other time. We are the ones we've been waiting for. We are the change that we seek.

~ Barack Obama ~

The evil shadow of racism has been one of America's darkest clouds. The election and subsequent reelection of Barack Obama as President were watershed events that healed some of the wounds of racism in America. The fact that Obama defeated a decorated war hero from a famous family of naval officers made the victory all the more impressive.

 **THOUGHT FOR TODAY:** While improvements must still be made to end the scourge of racism in American, the United States has made much progress toward racial equality.

NOVEMBER 5: INVESTIGATIVE JOURNALISM IS BORN

There is a choice for a man to make. He can choose the fair and open path, or choose the secret way by which he can get the better of his fellow man.

~ Ida Tarbell ~

Today is the birthday of Ida Tarbell, whose meticulously researched history of Rockefeller's Standard Oil birthed investigative journalism. Hampered by sexism and the secrecy of Standard Oil, Tarbell was undeterred. She gained the confidence of a company executive and pored over hundreds of documents. Her work was the catalyst for the breakup of Standard Oil and the downfall of a tycoon. In the century that followed her masterpiece, investigative journalists have established themselves as another check on the power of politicians, corporations and governments.

THOUGHT FOR TODAY: Some decry sensationalism in journalism, but many earnest and skilled journalists work hard to check the abuse of power by politicians and big business. When you see an investigative news story on TV, thank pioneers like Ida Tarbell, who created a genre that led to protective journalism.

NOVEMBER 6: NO STATIC AT ALL!

Technology gives us the facilities that lessen the barriers of time and distance - the telegraph and cable, the telephone, radio, and the rest.

~ Emily Greene Balch ~

On this day in 1935, Edwin Armstrong presented a paper entitled "A Method of Reducing Disturbances in Radio Signaling by a System of Frequency Modulation." What did this mean for radio listeners? Clearer, more beautiful FM radio. AM radio had been around for a while, but it often crackled with static, and the sound fidelity was poor. FM radio produced much less static and much better sound quality. It meant better reception and more clarity, especially for music. FM radio would come to define the life of Baby Boomers and provide pleasure for all radio listeners.

 **THOUGHT FOR TODAY:** Until very recently, few people had access to music beyond local folk tunes. Now we can choose from hundreds of thousands of songs and symphonies and listen to high fidelity recordings whenever we want.

NOVEMBER 7: NUCLEAR WEAPONS AND FALLOUT SHELTERS

(The B53 hydrogen bomb) is a Cold War relic — there's no continuing need for it. And (its dismantling) shows the direction of our future.

~ Dan Poneman ~

On this day in 1957, the report "Deterrence and Survival in the Nuclear Age" was presented to President Eisenhower. In the wake of Sputnik, the report recommended the US develop more nuclear weapons and build fallout shelters to protect civilians. Students from the 50s and 60s recall huddling under their desks to practice nuclear attack drills. Today there are no fallout shelters or nuclear attack drills because the Cold War nuclear standoff is over.

THOUGHT FOR TODAY: North Korea's actions are frightening and dangerous, but that country does not possess the hundreds of ICBMs that the USSR and US pointed at each other during the Cold War. The dismantling of thousands of nuclear weapons since the end of the Cold War means we are much less likely to use them.

NOVEMBER 8: REFORMER DOROTHY DAY

The greatest challenge of the day is how to bring about a revolution of the heart, a revolution which has to start with each one of us.

~ Dorothy Day ~

Before she earned fame as a reformer, Dorothy Day lived a Bohemian life in New York. She began her career working for radical newspapers. Day later converted to Catholicism and co-founded *The Catholic Worker* newspaper. It covered the plight of the poorest during the Great Depression and spawned the Catholic Worker Movement. Today, there are 245 Catholic Worker communities around the world that are dedicated to help those most in need.

Religion often does not live up to it lofty ideals, but the hypocrisy of some practitioners should not condemn whole religions. Many millions take religious teachings of love and compassion to heart and work with the downtrodden.

THOUGHT FOR TODAY: For most of human history, care of the sick and poor was slapdash. Today thousands of governmental, religious and nonprofit organizations help those who suffer the most.

NOVEMBER 9: CAPITAL PUNISHMENT ABOLISHED IN BRITAIN

I should not regret a fair and full trial of the entire abolition of capital punishment.

~ James Madison ~

At our best, we are a compassionate species; at our worst, we are cruel. These two tendencies meet with vigor in the laws and punishments devised in the ancient and medieval worlds. The Bible called for capital punishment when sacrificing to the wrong gods, false prophecy, gay sex, and even loss of virginity before marriage. Humans invented many brutal forms of execution, such as burning at the stake, breaking on the wheel, and the guillotine. Over the years more "humane" forms of execution evolved, including hanging, electrocution, and now lethal injection. In recent years, most countries have done away with capital punishment. On this day in 1998, Britain officially took this step.

THOUGHT FOR TODAY: Human history demonstrates a steady decline in human cruelty. Even in the United States, a capital punishment holdout, executions are less frequent.

NOVEMBER 10: SESAME STREET PREMIERS

Bad days happen to everyone, but when one happens to you, just keep doing your best and never let a bad day make you feel bad about yourself.

~ Big Bird ~

On this day in 1969, the iconic PBS program featuring Ernie, Burt, Grover, Oscar and Big Bird premiered. Many millions of children got a daily dose of developmentally appropriate education about numbers and letters through songs, skits and engaging characters. In addition to the Three Rs, *Sesame Street* has taken on tougher topics like diversity and death, homelessness and discrimination.

Economists Melissa Kearney and Phillip Levine[1] studied the effects of Sesame Street on children in the 1970s and found that those who tuned into the PBS children's program did better than those who did not, especially among boys, blacks and Latinos.

 **THOUGHT FOR TODAY:** Programs like Sesame Street reach out to the rich and poor alike to provide education and entertainment that makes a difference.

NOVEMBER 11: MAYFLOWER COMPACT SIGNED

We in the Presence of God and one another, covenant and combine ourselves together into a civil Body Politick, for our better Ordering and Preservation

~ The Mayflower Compact ~

On this day in 1620, the Saints and the Strangers—the Pilgrims—agreed to community guidelines for their life in New England. They did so aboard the *Mayflower* as it lay in anchor off the tip of Cape Cod. The Compact set out the rules for survival together in the New World.

This relatively new form of governance was becoming more and more common among Europeans, and it would be a progenitor of later laws drawn up by the governed in the English colonies. Our Constitution draws on a long heritage of such documents, including the English Constitution and Magna Carta.

THOUGHT FOR TODAY: As Americans enjoy their Thanksgiving meal this fall, they ought to consider the many gifts of the Pilgrims. Their Compact was a fundamental document in what would become American democracy.

NOVEMBER 12: REDUCE, REUSE...RELAUNCH!

Civilization as we know it has been defined by exploration.
It's part of our being; it's part of our moral fiber to go off and
explore.

~ Alan G. Poindexter ~

On this day in 1981, NASA launched Space Shuttle *Columbia* on Mission STS-2, the first time a manned spacecraft was launched into space twice. *Columbia* and the rest of the Shuttle fleet would go on back to space on 135 missions. While two of the missions failed tragically, the 30-year space program brought 180 satellites and other payloads into space, replenished and ferried astronauts to and from the International Space Station, and conducted hundreds of experiments.

While the shuttle program has been suspended, a constant human presence in space continues. The International Space Station is constantly manned with astronauts and cosmonauts.

THOUGHT FOR TODAY: In less than 100 years, humans learned to fly and then to go into space. Our understanding of our planet and the cosmos beyond has been rocketed forward by incredible advances in aeronautics and space flight.

NOVEMBER 13: MICKEY'S ALL WET

We keep moving forward, opening new doors, and doing new things, because we're curious and curiosity keeps leading us down new paths.

~ Walt Disney ~

On this date in 1940 Walt Disney released *Fantasia,* an animated kaleidoscope set to classical music. Children of all ages were delighted by images of dinosaurs evolving to the music of Igor Stravinsky, hippos and ostriches dancing a ballet, and Mickey Mouse flooding a sorcerer's castle.

Animation continues to delight audiences. It has even taken a more serious turn in recent movies like *Wall-E* and *Zootopia.* Animation is one of the many high-tech innovations that has expanded the horizons of entertainment and provided yet another canvas for the imagination of filmmakers.

 **THOUGHT FOR TODAY:** Just as Walt Disney Studios revolutionized animation in the mid-20th century, today we live in another golden age of animation guided by Dreamworks, Pixar, and its parent company, Walt Disney.

NOVEMBER 14: NELLIE BLY BEGINS HER BIG ADVENTURE

Energy rightly applied and directed will accomplish anything.

~ Nellie Bly ~

On this day in 1889, journalist Nelly Bly embarked on a round-the-world adventure. Her mission was to circumnavigate the globe in fewer than 80 days, in effect beating the time of Philias Fogg, the main character of Jules Verne's *Around the World in Eighty Days*. As a reporter for Joseph Pulitzer's *New York World*, Bly sent occasional dispatches for her newspaper. She arrived in New York in 72 days, a new record for global circumnavigation.

Bly's adventure was a daring one, made all the more incredible because of the sexism of the day. She was one of many women who was breaking out of traditional roles and following her own path, not one directed by men.

THOUGHT FOR TODAY: Our ability to travel has expanded exponentially, as has the freedom for women to pursue their own paths.

NOVEMBER 15: FAIRTRADE LABEL LAUNCHED IN THE NETHERLANDS

Fair Trade evokes a relationship between consumers and producers based on transparency, dialogue, and respect.

~ Bryant Terry ~

Free trade has not always been fair trade. The rich and powerful have often taken the lion's share of the benefits, leaving the poorer producers with a smaller cut. In recent decades, the Fair Trade movement has created structures to ensure that all parties get an equitable share of the profits. On this day in 1988, the first Fair Trade label, Max Havelaar, launched in the Netherlands.

Today more than 1.5 million workers and farmers are involved in the Fair Trade economy, and more than a thousand certified organizations operate in nearly 75 countries.

THOUGHT FOR TODAY: In recent years the economic well-being of the poor in developing countries has been considered more seriously by consumers in rich countries. This global concern for mutual benefit has been growing and will likely continue through the 21st Century.

NOVEMBER 16: A MESSAGE OF OPTIMISM, BROADCAST TO SPACE

Space: the final frontier.

~ Captain James Kirk ~

On this day in 1974, the Arecibo Radio Telescope in Puerto Rico broadcast a message to a group of stars 25,000 light years away. It was a neighborly "hello" to the nearby M13 Hercules Globular Cluster.

Humans have a mixed history of exploring new lands. The conquest that followed Columbus's "discovery" of America was a story of exploitation and disease. The Arecibo message was a greeting, not a threat. Our intentions in space going forward are peaceful, unlike the ships that sailed west from Europe circa 1492.

THOUGHT FOR TODAY: In the past we explored new lands to seek conquest and fortune. Today our peaceful explorations are driven by curiosity and a desire to discover. By treaty we have agreed not to claim lands beyond the earth, a departure from typical human behavior in the past.

NOVEMBER 17: THE VELVET REVOLUTION

Hope, in this deep and powerful sense, is not the same as joy that things are going well, but rather an ability to work for something because it is good.

~ Václav Havel ~

O this day in 1989, a student demonstration in Prague was quelled by riot police, and a revolution began. The next day and each following day more and more people marched against the government, famously mobbing Wenceslas Square in downtown Prague. In a few weeks the government would be toppled, and before the end of the year Václav Havel would be the democratically elected president of the Czech Republic.

Before 1989, the idea of democracy returning to Eastern Europe seemed far-fetched, but in short order nearly all of the former Soviet satellites would transition to democracy.

 **THOUGHT FOR TODAY:** We too often take democracy for granted, but three hundred years ago there were no democracies. Today more than half of all people live in democratic societies.

NOVEMBER 18: NONVIOLENT CIVIL DISOBEDIENCE

I distrust those people who know so well what God wants them to do, because I notice it always coincides with their own desires.

~ Susan B. Anthony ~

On this day in 1872, Susan B. Anthony and 14 other women were arrested for illegally voting in the US presidential election. Gandhi or Martin Luther King often come to mind when we think of nonviolent civil disobedience, but the suffragettes of the 1800s were pioneers in the art of protest.

For all but a tiny sliver of recent history, women had little autonomy and few rights. Anthony and the other women who protested were considered radical in their day, but, not for their bravery, women might never have earned legal equality.

THOUGHT FOR TODAY: Human rights continue to expand, thanks in part to the brave work of activists and revolutionaries like Susan B. Anthony, Mohandas Gandhi, Martin Luther King, and Nelson Mandela.

NOVEMBER 19: A NEW BIRTH OF FREEDOM

This nation, under God, shall have a new birth of freedom – and that government of the people, by the people, for the people, shall not perish from the earth.

~ Abraham Lincoln ~

On this day in 1863, Abraham Lincoln Delivered the Gettysburg Address. It was a speech to mark the dedication of a military cemetery in Pennsylvania, but the concise and eloquent Address became famous as a description of the values for which the Civil War was fought.

It is rather for us to be here dedicated to the great task remaining before us...that we here highly resolve that these dead shall not have died in vain – that this nation, under God, shall have a new birth of freedom – and that government of the people, by the people, for the people, shall not perish from the earth.

 **THOUGHT FOR TODAY:** The Civil War was America's deadliest war, but it ended slavery and brought about a new birth of freedom.

NOVEMBER 20: THE CUBAN MISSILE CRISIS ENDS

I look forward to a future in which our country will match its military strength with our moral restraint, its wealth with our wisdom, its power with our purpose.

~ John F. Kennedy ~

On this day in 1962, President John F. Kennedy ended the quarantine of Cuba. This blockade—called a quarantine for diplomatic reasons—forced Soviet Premier Nikita Khrushchev to withdraw missiles in from the Caribbean and thus end the Cuban Missile Crisis. For a few days in November, the world was close to a cataclysmic war.

After the fall of the Soviet Union, Russia and the United States have worked together to decrease the size of their nuclear arsenals. While a rogue state like North Korea might use a nuclear weapon, an exchange of missiles between major powers seems very, very unlikely.

THOUGHT FOR TODAY: We live in a world where none of the major powers is preparing to attack its adversary. We often forget that just a generation ago, the threat of nuclear war hung over the planet.

NOVEMBER 21: THOMAS EDISON RECORDS SOUND

Where words fail, music speaks.

~ Hans Christian Andersen ~

Imagine modern life without recorded sound. It is a part of everyday life, be it in a voicemail or your iPod, yet we have only had this capability for about 150 years. On this date in 1877, Thomas Edison announced his invention of the phonograph. Over the years he improved his designs such that the phonograph became a popular household item owned by millions.

Like many other inventions, the phonograph morphed into inexpensive, high quality, high capacity devices. Today's digital audio players hold thousands of songs of impeccable audio fidelity. Whether we prefer the Grateful Dead or Gregorian chant, access to high quality recordings is easy and inexpensive.

THOUGHT FOR TODAY: We live in an age of easy access to millions of songs, podcasts, and audiobooks to expand our mind and elevate our soul.

NOVEMBER 22: EVEN ANIMALS HAVE RIGHTS

I became a vegetarian after realizing that animals feel afraid, cold, hungry and unhappy like we do. I feel very deeply about vegetarianism and the animal kingdom.

~ César Chávez ~

In ancient and medieval times, abuse of animals was a form of entertainment. In ancient Rome, Augustus claimed to have had 3500 African animals killed in hunts conducted in arenas for entertainment. Bear baiting in Elizabethan England involving dogs attacking a bear in an enclosed area surrounded by cheering (and paying) spectators.

In the 1800s, organizations for the humane treatment of animals sprang up in Europe and the United States. On this day in 1954, the Humane Society of the United States was founded as an offshoot of the American Humane Society.

THOUGHT FOR TODAY: Today we give our pets loving care, but for most of history, animals were often abused for "entertainment." Our circle of compassion has expanded to animals. Pets have become members of our extended family.

NOVEMBER 23: FIRST FEMALE AFRICAN PRESIDENT

Of course, I am the first democratically elected woman president in Africa, and that raises a lot of expectations. I represent the aspirations of women all over Africa.

~ Ellen Johnson Sirleaf ~

On this day in 2005, Ellen Johnson Sirleaf was elected president of Liberia and became the first woman to head an African country. Africa was treated particularly badly at the hands of European slavers and colonists, so it is no surprise that many African countries have been slow to develop stable, inclusive institutions. Nonetheless, progress has been increasing. Today more African nations are democratic than at any other time in history.

Sirleaf was awarded the Nobel Peace Prize in 2011 for her efforts to bring peace, promote development, and improve the position of women.

THOUGHT FOR TODAY: Many westerners still see sub-Saharan Africa as a failing region of the world, but many countries are developing rapidly, with significant improvements in health, democracy and education.

NOVEMBER 24: ORIGIN OF SPECIES IS PUBLISHED

In the long history of humankind (and animal kind, too) those who learned to collaborate and improvise most effectively have prevailed.

~ Charles Darwin ~

On this day in 1859, Charles Darwin's most famous book was published in Britain. It was drawn from careful observations made as science officer of *HMS Beagle*. Darwin's time in the Galapagos Islands was especially influential in shaping his theory of evolution, an idea that has stood the test of time and formed the foundation of our understanding of life.

THOUGHT FOR TODAY: When you consider the beauty and splendor of the natural world, think about how Darwin and others have enriched our understanding of it. This knowledge has led to better farming techniques, veterinary medicine, and human health advances. Just as species evolve into more and more complex organisms, so too does our understanding of the natural world.

NOVEMBER 25: GREAT AMERICAN PHILANTHROPISTS

No man will make a great leader who wants to do it all himself, or to get all the credit for doing it.

~ Andrew Carnegie ~

On this day in 1835, Andrew Carnegie was born in Dunfermline, Scotland. He embodied the American dream. After Carnegie emigrated to America, he built a steel company and became a millionaire. Carnegie sold the company and spent the rest of his life being a philanthropist. He founded 2000 public libraries, Carnegie-Mellon University, and an endowment for world peace, among other projects.

Andrew Carnegie became an example of how a tycoon can make the world a better place by giving wisely to philanthropic organizations. He is a precursor to modern philanthropists like Bill and Melinda Gates, who have saved millions of lives through the good works of their foundation.

THOUGHT FOR TODAY: In ancient times, the rich and powerful sought only to enrich themselves. Today more and more philanthropists are seeking to help those who have the least.

NOVEMBER 26: BILL WILSON BORN IN VERMONT

It must never be forgotten that the purpose of Alcoholics Anonymous is to sober up alcoholics. There is no religious or spiritual requirement for membership.

~ Bill Wilson ~

As long as there has been alcohol there have been alcoholics. These people—colloquially described as drunks, dipsomaniacs, lushes, and sots—often led slow deaths of public disgrace and private heartbreak. One social movement that created a successful route out of the hell of addiction is Alcoholics Anonymous (AA).

On this day in 1895, Bill Wilson was born in Vermont. After a promising career on Wall Street, he, like the economy, crashed and burned. In 1935 he met Bob Smith and founded the fellowship that has helped millions get sober.

THOUGHT FOR TODAY: Mutual aid societies have emerged to help people overcome difficult struggles and find support for personal strength. Thanks to social movements like AA, and medical advances in addiction treatment, there are many ways out of the sick and dispiriting hole of addiction.

NOVEMBER 27: JAMES PRATT AND JOHN SMITH EXECUTED

Why is it that, as a culture, we are more comfortable seeing two men holding guns than holding hands?

~ Ernest J. Gaines ~

Today same-sex marriage is legal in at least 25 countries. But less than two hundred years ago, men were still being executed for engaging in gay sex. On this day in 1835, James Pratt and John Smith were publicly hanged at Newgate Prison after being found guilty of "sodomy."

Progress in LGBT equality has been very slow, and prejudice and persecution are still too common. In parts of the world men can still be executed for homosexuality. Nevertheless, the growth of LGBT rights has accelerated in recent years.

 **THOUGHT FOR TODAY:** We have made much progress toward LGBT equality, especially in recent years. In fits and starts, LGBT rights have expanded, and in more than 25 countries, people can marry whomever they love, regardless of their sex.

NOVEMBER 28: THE FIRST KING OF MOTOWN

Don't judge yourself by others' standards…have your own.
And don't get caught up into the trap of changing yourself to
fit the world. The world has to change to fit you.

~ Berry Gordy ~

On this day in 1929, business pioneer Berry Gordy was born in Georgia. His distant cousin Jimmy Carter would stay in Georgia and eventually become president, but Gordy's family moved north to Detroit, the Motor City.

In the late 1950s, Gordy met singer Jackie Wilson, who recorded some songs co-written by Gordy and his sister Gwen. The songs became hits, and Gordy built a music company that would become Motown Records. Motown would produce records for successful acts like the Miracles, the Supremes, the Temptations, the Commodores, Stevie Wonder and the Jackson 5.

THOUGHT FOR TODAY: Centuries of prejudice meant that it was difficult for people of color to break into businesses. Pioneers like Madame C.J. Walker and Berry Gordy broke down barriers that made way for Robert Johnson, Oprah Winfrey and other self-made African American entrepreneurs.

NOVEMBER 29: PONG BOUNCES ONTO SCREENS

If you are a gamer, it's time to get over any regret you might feel. You have been building up a wealth of virtual experience that can teach you about your true self.

~ Jane McGonigal ~

On this day in 1972, Atari announced the release of Pong, the first successful video game. The viral spread and success of Pong led to the rapid development of other video games and the gaming industry. In 2016 the video gaming industry generated more than $30 billion in revenue.

People debate the pros and cons of video games, but they certainly bring joy to hundreds of millions of people around the world. And recent studies suggest that gaming can improve coordination, problem-solving skills, and attention and concentration.

 **THOUGHT FOR TODAY:** Entertainment options have multiplied in recent decades such that there is something for everyone to enjoy, be it multi-player video games or Words With Friends.

NOVEMBER 30: MADD TIES ONE ON FOR SAFETY

Death by drink driving is the only socially acceptable form of homicide.

~ Candy Lightner ~

Mothers Against Drunk Driving (MADD) started to advocate for public awareness about and stricter penalties for drunk driving. In 1980, its founding year, there were approximately 25,000 drunk driving fatalities each year. Now the number is a about 10,000...a tragic statistic, but that's 15,000 fewer deaths than in 1980. MADD estimates that its efforts have saved 330,000 lives.

THOUGHT FOR TODAY: When you pass a police car on the road, remember that rates of driving under the influence of alcohol have decreased. So too have the number of deaths caused by intoxicated drivers. The numerous nonprofit advocacy organizations that fight societal problems like drunk driving are often very successful. The existence of groups like MADD are a force for good in our modern age.

DECEMBER 1: ROSA PARKS KEEPS HER SEAT

I have learned over the years that when one's mind is made up, this diminishes fear; knowing what must be done does away with fear.

~ Rosa Parks ~

On this day in 1955, Rosa Parks refused to give up her bus seat to a white passenger. This act of civil disobedience precipitated a yearlong boycott of Montgomery, Alabama buses by the black community. The boycott led to the emergence of a young Martin Luther King. The US Supreme Court sided with Parks and determined that segregation on buses was unconstitutional. Her disobedience to unfair laws is now seen as a heroic act against discrimination, and she is an inspiration to all who fight racism.

THOUGHT FOR TODAY: Injustices exist everywhere, even in democracies, but we can fight for right by using nonviolent protest and mobilizing the public. Rosa Parks reminds us that small acts of righteous defiance can change the world for the better.

DECEMBER 2: EPA IS FOUNDED

Plans to protect air and water, wilderness and wildlife are in fact plans to protect man.

~ Stewart Udall ~

On this day in 1970, the Environmental Protection Agency (EPA) was founded. The state of the environment was so bad by 1970 that legislators on both sides of the aisle agreed that something drastic must be done. The creation of the EPA was a bipartisan effort signed by a Republican president. Since the founding of the EPA, there has been much progress, including reductions in auto emissions, the banning of DDT, and the cleanup of toxic waste. Environmental laws like the Clean Air and Clean Water Acts set standards that led to a healthier environment.

THOUGHT FOR TODAY: Before 1970, factories billowed noxious black smoke and cars pumped lead, a pernicious neurotoxin, into the atmosphere. Thanks to the EPA and new environmental rules, the environment in the United States has become much cleaner since the founding of the EPA.

DECEMBER 3: FIRST HUMAN HEART TRANSPLANT

The human body experiences a powerful gravitational pull in the direction of hope. That is why the patient's hopes are the physician's secret weapon.

~ Norman Cousins ~

In ancient and medieval times, a trip to the surgeon was often deadlier than the disease that brought you there. In the last 150 years, surgical techniques and procedures have improved by leaps and bounds. One milestone was the first successful heart transplant, which happened on this day in 1967. Today thousands of heart transplants are performed in the world each year. Currently, survival rates for the first five years after transplant are better than 65%.

THOUGHT FOR TODAY: Today we benefit from medical techniques that were the stuff of science fiction just a few generations ago. The rate and lethality of heart attacks has been falling because of breakthroughs like statin drugs, blood thinners, and effective and less invasive surgeries. These innovations prolong life and improve its quality.

DECEMBER 4: THE NATIONAL GRANGE IS FOUNDED

At the core, labor unions are working men and women, unified as one force; we have banded together to protect and improve the lives of workers.

~ Sue Carney ~

The rich and powerful have always been able to pull the strings in their favor. In the 19th century, workers organizations and labor unions began to push back. One organization, the National Grange of the Order of Patrons of Husbandry, had its first meeting on this day in 1867. The Grange was founded to promote the interests of farmers and rural communities. It succeeded in getting farmers better rates with the monopolistic railroads and better rural mail delivery. Today the Grange has more than 100,000 members.

THOUGHT FOR TODAY: Community organizations connect us, give us support, and provide ways for all of us to flourish. This rich web of community resources is a relatively new development. Consider connecting with a community group to improve your life and make the world a better place.

DECEMBER 5: THE BIG SMOKE OF LONDON

One of the pillars of backward thinking in America is the idea that you can have jobs or you can have clean air and water, but you can't have both.

~ Jeff Goodell ~

O n this day in 1952, the Great Smog descended on London. Its cause was the coal used to heat homes and run factories. This period of severe air pollution sickened about 100,000, and some suggest it killed as many as 12,000 Britons.

Most people think air pollution is a recent problem, but this is wrong. London's air quality had been bad since at least 1200. In the past, people burned wood or coal, fuels that poison the air with soot, carbon monoxide, and smoke.

THOUGHT FOR TODAY: It is often forgotten that we live in an age of clean fuels. Homes are often heated with natural gas, the cleanest of carbon fuels. In much of the world, air quality is much better than it was in the past, thanks to sensible regulations and clean air technologies.

DECEMBER 6: SPAIN RATIFIES A NEW CONSTITUTION

Man's capacity for justice makes democracy possible, but man's inclination to injustice makes democracy necessary.

~ Reinhold Niebuhr ~

Francisco Franco was one of many fascist rulers in the 20th century. In 1940, fascism and communism were on a roll. After World War II, fascism was discredited, but Franco's Spain was a holdout.

One of many turning points toward democracy in Spain happened after the death of Franco in 1975. His successor, King Juan Carlos, was expected to continue the fascist government, but instead he installed Adolfo Suárez to lead a transition to democracy. Suárez tread a delicate balance as he tried to avoid another civil war, which had preceded the rise of Franco. On this day in 1978 the constitution that established Spanish democracy was ratified.

THOUGHT FOR TODAY: The worst forms of authoritarianism—fascism and communism—have fared poorly in the last 70 years. Today more than half of the world's people live in democracies.

DECEMBER 7: MEASURING THE SPEED OF LIGHT

Those who would legislate against the teaching of evolution should also legislate against gravity, electricity and the unreasonable velocity of light.

~ Luther Burbank ~

Humans have attempted to understand the properties of light, but people found it difficult to measure its properties. On this day in 1676, Danish astronomer Ole Rømer's calculations of the speed of light were presented in *Journal des Sçavans*.

How does one measure the speed of light in the 1600s? Rømer observed the eclipse of Jovian moons at different times of year and determined the time discrepancies between the observations. From this he hypothesized that light travels 214,000 kilometers per second. While he was off by 30%, he did posit compelling proof of the finite speed of light.

THOUGHT FOR TODAY: Science continuously removes the shroud of unknowing from timeless mysteries. Thanks to these advances, we come to better understand the universe and find ways to make our lives better.

DECEMBER 8: A WOMAN PLAYS A WOMAN

A bird doesn't sing because it has an answer, it sings because it has a song.

~ Maya Angelou ~

On this day in 1660, a woman played a woman onstage. This was a big deal. In Shakespeare's day and after his death, men played the female roles because acting was deemed inappropriate for women. But after the Restoration, Charles II allowed women onstage. We are not sure who the first woman actress was, but we do know that she played Desdemona in *Othello*.

It is hard to imagine that sexism prevented actresses from plying their craft, but such was the world for most of human history. Today, barriers for women still exist but are subtler, and we are making progress toward ending sex discrimination.

 **THOUGHT FOR TODAY:** For much of history women could not play a leading role in public performance. After too many years of male dominance, the arts are opening to women.

DECEMBER 9: IPHONES AND APOLLO ROCKETS?

Humans are allergic to change. They love to say, "We've always done it this way." I try to fight that. That's why I have a clock on my wall that runs counter-clockwise.

~ Grace Hopper ~

Many consider putting men on the moon to be the greatest achievement of humanity, for good reason. Yet do you know you have a rocket in your pocket? Let's compare the iPhone to the Apollo computer system.

Number of transistors – The iPhone has 130,000 times more than Apollo.

Instructions per second – The iPhone is 80,800,000 times faster than Apollo.

Overall performance – The iPhone is 120,000,000 times faster than Apollo.

Smartphones and other mobile devices connect, entertain, remind, record, play music, and photograph. These devices, when used prudently, make life easier and richer.

THOUGHT FOR TODAY: One hundred years ago, we had no computers. Fifty years ago, they took up whole rooms. The smart phone in your hand replaces dozens of separate items, including camera, portable music player, telephone, flashlight, GPS, calendar and other things that we once purchase separately.

DECEMBER 10: FIRST NOBEL PRIZES AWARDED

If I have a thousand ideas and only one turns out to be good, I am satisfied.

~ Alfred Nobel ~

Alfred Nobel was a Swedish inventor and businessman who held more than 355 patents. In his day he was famous for inventing dynamite. Upon reading a premature obituary that condemned him as a merchant of death, Nobel decided to bequeath his fortune to establish prizes for accomplishments in the sciences and literature.

Like many tycoons, Nobel realized that money is not the sole end of human existence, and today he is known—like Carnegie, Rockefeller, and Gates—for generosity as much as affluence.

 **THOUGHT FOR TODAY:** If you reflect on the great minds of our day, many of them, like Albert Einstein, Martin Luther King, and Mother Theresa, are Nobel laureates. In the 21st century, the greatest honors go to the greatest inventors, peacemakers, and poets, not to warriors and plutocrats.

DECEMBER 11: UNICEF FOUNDED

I can testify to what UNICEF means to children because I was among those who received food and medical relief right after World War II.

~ Audrey Hepburn ~

On this day in 1946, the United Nations International Children's Emergency Fund (UNICEF) was founded. It was created to help mothers and children receive food and health services in the wake of the devastation of World War II. By 1950 some six million children were receiving daily meals thanks to their efforts. In the 1980s, UNICEF focused on proven health interventions like breastfeeding, immunizations and oral rehydration therapy. UNICEF's efforts to make the world better for the next generation were acknowledged with the 1965 Nobel Peace Prize.

THOUGHT FOR TODAY: In 1900, more than a third of children died in the first five years of life. Today, according to Max Roser of Our World in Data, fewer than 5% do. The work of UNICEF and many other organizations has reduced infant mortality levels around the world.

DECEMBER 12: KENYA GAINS INDEPENDENCE

Our children may learn about heroes of the past. Our task is to make ourselves architects of the future.

~ Jomo Kenyatta ~

In 1963, Kenya gained independence from its colonial overlord, Great Britain. The 60s were an era of decolonization after World War II; dozens of countries in Asia and Africa gained freedom from their (mostly) European overlords. This period is also unique because in the past, great powers had never given up imperial possessions because it was the right thing to do. While most of the colonies had native anti-colonial movements, decolonization was necessary because European powers espoused democratic values.

 **THOUGHT FOR TODAY:** Since World War II, European overlords have allowed former colonies to be free. Today few countries are ruled by foreign powers. Decolonization was the triumph of self-determination. We live in an era where ethical considerations are crowding out age-old Machiavellian considerations.

DECEMBER 13: AMERICAN IN PARIS PREMIERES

A song is not a song until you sing it

A bell is not a bell until you ring it

Love is not Love until you give it away

~ George Gershwin ~

On this day in 1928, George Gershwin's jazz orchestral masterpiece *An American in Paris* debuted. Classical composers had been borrowing folk melodies for their music for a long time, a process that accelerated during the romantic 1800s. Gershwin's large-scale works, like *Rhapsody in Blue* and *Porgy and Bess*, beautifully bridged American jazz and European classical music. Gershwin's great works are now orchestral standards around the globe.

THOUGHT FOR TODAY: Music and all the arts continue to mix and morph, diversify and disperse. Many different kinds of music fill our ears nowadays, from pop, soul, and hip hop; to classical, jazz, and reggae. Thanks to the global interconnectedness of cultures, we have never had such a rich panoply of music. We are blessed to have access, via digital platforms, to all the music ever created by humanity.

DECEMBER 14: THE DAYTON AGREEMENT IS SIGNED

The Peace Agreement succeeded in what it set to achieve—
it ended a conflict and provided a starting point for
negotiations and cooperation.

~ Lana Pasic ~

The Balkans were once synonymous with intractable ethnic strife. Marshal Broz Tito kept diverse Yugoslavia unified—and prevented violence—by maintaining an iron grip on power. Once the Cold War ended and Yugoslavia split apart, the Balkans became engulfed in war. But thanks to diplomacy, on this day in 1995 the Dayton Agreement brought peace back to the former Yugoslavia.

The Dayton Agreement successfully ended most of the Balkan conflicts. The Kosovo War in the late 90s were a bloody setback. Nonetheless, the Dayton Agreement stabilized a region that had been the birthplace of wars, including World War I.

 **THOUGHT FOR TODAY:** Considering its history, it is incredible that there hasn't been war in the Balkans in the 21st century. The Dayton Agreement is evidence that diplomacy can end conflicts that once seemed intractable.

DECEMBER 15: RIGHTS GUARANTEED

Liberty must at all hazards be supported. We have a right to it, derived from our Maker. But if we had not, our fathers have earned and bought it for us

~ John Adams ~

On this day in 1791, the US Bill of Rights became law when it was ratified by the Virginia General Assembly. These first ten amendments to the Constitution were added because of the vociferous protests of those who feared government overreach. The Bill guaranteed personal rights, freedoms and limitations on government power. It rested on important precursors, including the Virginia Declaration of Rights and the medieval Magna Carta. Today most countries have constitutions that limit government power and guarantee human rights.

THOUGHT FOR TODAY: Our rights are guaranteed and vouchsafed by constitutional protections. The Bill of Rights was a radical innovation in its time. It codified a humane vision of legal equality, protection and freedom. Around the world most humans enjoy protections delineated in the Bill of Rights.

DECEMBER 16: BEETHOVEN'S GENIUS

Don't only practice your art, but force your way into its secrets; art deserves that, for it and knowledge can raise man to the Divine.

~ Ludwig van Beethoven ~

Few figures in history strike as bold a figure as Beethoven. As a young man he moved to Vienna to study with Haydn. Beethoven established himself as a piano virtuoso and then an eminent composer. Despite these successes, he suffered from self-doubt and hearing loss.

Beethoven's works, notably his heroic symphonies and piano concertos, have inspired millions around the world. His music reminds us of the depth of human emotion, expression, creativity and achievement.

THOUGHT FOR TODAY: While he suffered bouts of depression and was deaf at the end of his life, Beethoven's creative vitality and ultimate faith in humanity—expressed in the Ode to Joy in his final symphony—transcended his struggles. When we struggle, let us be inspired by works of genius and beauty.

DECEMBER 17: LIFTOFF AT KITTY HAWK

If we all worked on the assumption that what is accepted as true is really true, there would be little hope of advance.

~ Orville Wright ~

On this day in 1903, the Wright Brothers' heavier-than-air Flyer soared above the sands of Kitty Hawk, North Carolina. This achievement seemed promising but not particularly auspicious. The first flight lasted only 12 seconds and spanned a mere 120 feet, a third of a football field. But the Wrights persisted. The fourth and final flight of the day lasted 59 seconds and spanned nearly three football fields.

THOUGHT FOR TODAY: When you see a jet flying high above you, recall that our great-grandparents could not fly to other cities and countries, something that is now routine. Today millions of people fly more than a billion miles each day, thanks to the discoveries of the Wrights and thousands of aeronautical innovators that followed their first flights.

DECEMBER 18: STEVE BIKO

Man, you are okay as you are. Begin to look upon yourself as a human being.

~ Steve Biko ~

The fight against apartheid had many heroes and martyrs, including Steve Biko. He founded the South African Students' Organization in the late 60s and was the architect of the Black Consciousness movement in his country. Biko insisted on working in solidarity with all non-whites in South Africa, all of whom were victims of apartheid.

By 1973 the apartheid government banned him from travel and public speeches, but in 1977 he traveled to Cape Town. On his way back to his hometown, Biko was detained, interrogated and beaten. He eventually died of his injuries. His martyrdom galvanized opposition to apartheid.

THOUGHT FOR TODAY: The world may seem full of evil, yet crusaders live Steve Biko live—and sometimes die—for causes greater than themselves. Many of these causes, like the fight against apartheid, are victorious in the end.

DECEMBER 19: THE BRITISH GIVE UP HONG KONG

Life in Hong Kong transcends cultural and culinary borders, such that nothing is truly foreign and nothing doesn't belong.

~ Peter Jon Lindberg ~

In ancient times, empires never ceded their conquests. Such generosity would have been seen as weakness. But in the 20th century, great powers around the world were giving up colonies they had conquered or stolen.

The United Kingdom wrested Hong Kong from China as one of its spoils from the Opium War, a particularly cynical episode in Britain's history of imperial ventures. Nonetheless, the United Kingdom and China negotiated an agreement whereby Hong Kong was returned to China. In return, Hong Kong was allowed to keep much of its autonomy.

THOUGHT FOR TODAY: We live in the most peaceful age in human history, a time when empires could take over smaller powers, but new norms of international behavior deem old imperial ways unacceptable and unethical.

DECEMBER 20: MÉDECINS SANS FRONTIÈRES

The people who have impressed me most - and the closest
I've come to having heroes - are the people who have
devoted their lives to making things better for others.

~ *Bruce Cockburn* ~

On this day in 1971, the international organization Doctors Without Borders—Médecins Sans Frontières (MSF) in French—was created. MSF started in response to the Biafra War in Nigeria. Since then MSF doctors and medical professionals have treated more than a hundred million patients.

The organization has grown exponentially. In recent years more than 36,000 workers in some 70 countries participated, mostly as volunteers, in international projects. In 1999 the organization was awarded the Nobel Peace Prize for its humanitarian accomplishments.

 **THOUGHT FOR TODAY:** After World War II, volunteer organizations such as Médecins Sans Frontières have proliferated in response to humanitarian needs. At no time in history have so many given so much to make the world a better, safer and healthier place.

DECEMBER 21: THE ROCHDALE PIONEERS BAND TOGETHER

Co-operative enterprises provide the organizational means whereby humanity is able to take into its own hands the tasks of achieving social integration.

~ Boutros Boutros-Ghali ~

The modern cooperative movement began in England on this day in 1844. The Rochdale pioneers, a group of ten weavers and twenty others, created a cooperative food store because monopolistic producers were making everyday items too expensive. They adopted The Rochdale Principles, ideals for cooperative management that still inform and inspire cooperative movements to this day.

Electrical, agricultural, and food co-ops still exist in the US, and credit unions are a powerful force in American finance. In other countries, such as Denmark and Germany, cooperatives play an even bigger role in the economy.

THOUGHT FOR TODAY: There are thousands of cooperative organizations in each country and around the world. Coops give consumers more power and choice.

DECEMBER 22: WAŁĘSA ELECTED PRESIDENT OF POLAND

Tomorrow there will be no division to Europe and Asia.
These are old concepts that would remain only on maps.

~ Lech Wałęsa ~

An electrician at the Lenin Shipyard in Gdansk, Lech Wałęsa became a trade union activist in communist Poland. He co-founded the Solidarity movement in his country and was awarded the Nobel Peace Prize. When the Polish communist government fell, he became Poland's first democratically elected.

For much of the 20th century, it seemed like authoritarian communist states were a permanent part of the international landscape. Instead, everyday people like Lech Wałęsa defied authoritarianism overthrew dictatorships. Wałęsa's story reminds us that struggle against oppression often bears the fruits of human progress and liberty.

THOUGHT FOR TODAY: Remember that only a generation ago, the world was caught in an East-West deadlock where nuclear missiles were aimed at the USSR and US. Since the fall of communism, many countries that were once captive to the USSR are now free and democratic.

DECEMBER 23: AROUND THE WORLD ON ONE TANK OF GAS

A lot of people think that all the things that could be invented have been invented. But we are just on the frontier of discovery and invention. It's a very exciting time.

~ Dick Rutan ~

On this day in 1986, the Rutan Voyager landed where it had taken off after a nonstop flight of more than nine days and 26,000 miles. This marathon flight marked the first nonstop round-the-world flight.

Just as we worry about our wasteful ways, innovators strive to create new designs that expand our horizons with a smaller ecological footprint. Their efforts demonstrate both our creative drive and our desire to live within our means on planet earth.

THOUGHT FOR TODAY: When you step onto a bus or get behind the wheel of a car, remember that our vehicles have become more technologically sophisticated and fuel efficient. Today more and more cares are hybrid and electric. And many countries are mandating that future cars produce zero greenhouse gas emissions.

DECEMBER 24: EARTHRISE PHOTO

To see the earth as it truly is, small and blue and beautiful
in that eternal silence where it floats, is to see ourselves as
riders on the earth together

~ Archibald MacLeish ~

O*h my God! Look at that picture over there! There's the Earth coming up. Wow, is that pretty.*

The now famous Earthrise photo was snapped on Christmas Eve, 1968, as Apollo 8 astronauts orbited the moon. These and other astronauts were the first to experience a new phenomenon, the overview effect, the experience of seeing Earth from space. When astronauts view the earth from space, the experience a sense of the beauty, unity and fragility of their home planet.

From space, national boundaries vanish, the conflicts that divide people seem trivial, and the drive to protect this "pale blue dot" becomes both obvious and imperative.

THOUGHT FOR TODAY: From high above, the earth is a beautiful blue marble with no political divisions. Thanks to the overview effect, we can see that all humanity is bound together.

DECEMBER 25: HALLEY'S COMET, RIGHT ON SCHEDULE

Scarce any problem will appear more hard and difficult, than that of determining the distance of the Sun from the Earth very near the truth.

~ Edmond Halley ~

On Christmas Day in 1758, Halley's Comet was sighted by Johann Georg Palitzsch, which confirmed Edmund Halley's prediction of its return in 75 years after its previous visit. This was the first time a comet's passage was accurately predicted.

Today we not only predict and monitor comets, we fly satellites near them and explore their properties (see January 2). The long line of astronomers from ancient times through Halley to today have opened up the secrets of the universe.

THOUGHT FOR TODAY: Thanks to a long line of dedicated astronomers, we have mapped, explored and sent ships into space to plumb the many mysteries of space. We know more than ever about the origins of the universe, earth and ourselves. What great discoveries lie in our future?

DECEMBER 26: THE CURIES ANNOUNCE A DISCOVERY

Nothing in life is to be feared, it is only to be understood.
Now is the time to understand more, so that we may fear
less.

~ Marie Curie ~

Marie and Pierre Curie were a scientific team that made several significant breakthroughs. On this day in 1898 they announced their discovery of radium. Through a series of complicated investigations and difficult chemical processes, they isolated the element. Pierre proved that radium damaged living flesh, a discovery that gave rise to the use of radiation to kill cancer cells. For their efforts, the Curies won the Nobel Prize, though in some places Marie was not allowed to speak about her scientific work because of her sex.

THOUGHT FOR TODAY: At the turn of the 20th century, the Curies made discoveries that would save millions of lives, though they would sacrifice their own because of radiation poisoning. Marie Curie was the victim of much discrimination in her day. Today women make up approximately 40% of chemical and material scientists.

DECEMBER 27: THE FIRST FEMALE RABBI

If I confess what motivated me, a woman, to become a rabbi, two things come to mind. My belief in God's calling and my love of humans.

~ Regina Jonas ~

For millennia, women in Judaism and other religions were seen as lesser, unclean and a source of sin. But in the 19th and 20th centuries, as women gained civil and political rights, the male monopoly on religious authority began to melt. In the US, women were ordained in Free Will Baptist, Congregationalist, Wesleyan Methodist Connection, and Universalist churches. The pace of female ordination quickened in the 20th century, and in December 1935, Regina Jonas became the first female rabbi.

THOUGHT FOR TODAY: Today nearly all Protestant and Jewish denominations allow women to be ministers, priests or rabbis. Like all other professions, the clergy is finally opening up to women. While there is still much work to do to make the world fair and equitable for women, increased female leadership in all fields shows how far we've come.

DECEMBER 28: PROTECTION AGAINST EXTINCTION

Nothing is more priceless and more worthy of preservation than the rich array of animal life with which our country has been blessed.

~ Richard Nixon ~

On this day in 1971, President Richard Nixon signed the Endangered Species Act (ESA) into law. ESA was a great success, bringing back many species, such as the alligator, grizzly bear, gray wolf, California condor, peregrine falcon, and bald eagle.

Humans have been hunting animals to extinction since paleolithic times. Only today have we tried to reverse the trend of species extinction via programs like the endangered species acts.

THOUGHT FOR TODAY: Take time to reflect on the many species brought back from the brink of extinction, including the gray wolf, grizzly bear, and bald eagle. While we must do more to prevent species extinction, it is amazing that we care so much for other creatures that we have stringent laws protecting wild animals.

DECEMBER 29: IRISH FREE STATE BECOMES IRELAND

We have played our part in the perseverance, and we have pledged ourselves to the dead generations who have preserved intact for us this glorious heritage.

~ Eamon de Valera ~

For some 800 years, England and later the United Kingdom would rule Ireland. In the early 20th century, the Catholic majority in the south successfully rebelled against Great Britain and gained effective independence. On this day in 1937, the people of the Irish Free State voted to become an independent country, Éire. It has been a democracy for its entire history. In recent decades it has shaken its reputation as a poor corner of Europe. Its newly vibrant economy is an apt counterpart to an Irish culture heritage that has been vibrant for millennia.

THOUGHT FOR TODAY: Nearly all colonial dominions shake off their overlords, and Ireland—despite 800 years of rule from London—eventually gained its freedom and independence.

DECEMBER 30: THE FIGHT AGAINST MALARIA

There will be statues of Bill Gates across the Third World. There's a reasonable shot that - because of his money - we will cure malaria.

~ Malcolm Gladwell ~

Malaria has been pestering humans for at least ten thousand years. In recent centuries scientists have made inroads to treat it. Female Chinese scientist Tu Youyou, who was born this day in 1930, studied traditional Chinese medicine and discovered artemisinin to be an effective treatment for malaria. Her discovery has saved millions of lives, and in 2015 she shared the Nobel Prize for Medicine and Physiology for her work.

In recent times public health programs have reduced malaria sickness and death in much of the world. Current efforts are underway to eradicate malaria, and human ingenuity will someday end this timeless scourge.

 **THOUGHT FOR TODAY:** What's the deadliest animal? No, it isn't the shark, tiger or snake; it's the mosquito. But thanks to thousands of scientists like Tu Youyou, we are getting the upper hand on mosquito-borne illness.

DECEMBER 31: THE END OF A GREAT GIFT

All of humankind will envision a global agenda that encompasses a kind of Global Marshall Plan to address the causes of environmental destruction all over the earth.

~ Al Gore ~

In days past, nations that were victorious in war pillaged, looted and despoiled the vanquished. After World War II, the United States did the opposite: It committed to the reconstruction of its enemies. The most famous of these programs was the Marshall Plan, a successful effort that restarted Germany's economic engine. Germany turned its back on a history of aggressive militarism. Today the country is a force for peace and stability, thanks in part to the generosity of the Marshall Plan. Today is also George Marshall's birthday (1880).

THOUGHT FOR TODAY: Interstate wars are uncommon in the 21st century, as are civil wars and genocides. This is due in part because the great powers are committed to creating a safer world governed by the rule of law.

Made in the USA
Monee, IL
23 December 2019

19494939R00212